SUNDAY MORNING:
THE NEW WAY

SUNDAY MORNING:

THE NEW WAY

Papers on the Parish Communion

EDITED BY

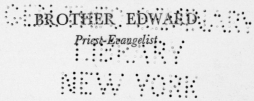

BROTHER EDWARD

Priest-Evangelist

"Brethren, I write no new Commandment unto you,
but an old Commandment which ye had from the
beginning."—1 St. John 2. 7.

LONDON

SOCIETY FOR PROMOTING
CHRISTIAN KNOWLEDGE

NORTHUMBERLAND AVENUE, W.C.2

NEW YORK: THE MACMILLAN COMPANY

First published 1938

WHAT IS MEANT BY THE PARISH COMMUNION?

" By ' the Parish Communion ' is meant the celebration of the Holy Eucharist with the communion of the people, in a parish church, as the chief service of the day, or, better, as the assembly of the Christian community for the worship of God."[1] This book contains a series of descriptions of the Parish Communion as it actually exists to-day, in a variety of parishes, " high," " moderate," and " low," in town, suburb, building-estate, village, and in the mission-field, presenting diverse embodiments in diverse material of one ruling idea: for " the unity of the holy Church of God is not divided by distance of place nor by diversity of traditions and ceremonies diversely observed in divers churches, for good order of the same."[2]

[1] *The Parish Communion*, p. 3.   [2] *The King's Book*, 1543.

PREFACE

THERE once was a child who said to her mother, "Mother, I think I should understand if only you wouldn't explain."

This little book is not meant to explain. It is written by parish priests who tell, each in his own way, of things that God has wrought among their people.

There is need for explanation; and the theological groundwork has been admirably laid by the writers of *The Parish Communion* (edited by A. G. Hebert, S.S.M.; S.P.C.K., 1937, 7s. 6d.). The descriptions in this book may serve as pictures between the leaves of that more learned volume.

I feel I owe an apology for undertaking the editorship; for I am not a man of letters. But I have had rather exceptional opportunities of seeing the Parish Eucharist at work in many parishes, both in town and country. I was present at Temple Balsall in 1913 at a Mission, conducted by Fr. Seyzinger, C.R., when he and the Vicar, Fr. Fairbairn, were led to make this innovation, as it then was, with the most blessed results.[1] Some of us look to Temple Balsall as the Jerusalem of this movement.[2] It was then that I saw in action what I had for years longed for, but had

[1] A description will be found in *The Parish Communion*, pp. 257–68.
[2] A beginning had been made earlier in other places: *e.g.*, Easterton, Wilts. (1874), Perth (Scotland), Sydney (New South Wales) and at St. Saviour's, Poplar.

believed to be impracticable—the union of the offering and the Communion with dignity and at the same time with simplicity, together with a happy and a holy gathering of the spiritual family at the breakfast afterwards. Since then I have watched this take place in parish after parish, very often (but not always) successfully. We must never think of this thing as a "stunt," or a bright idea for "getting people to church." If it is anything, it is a mighty movement of the Holy Spirit; and the devil opposes tooth and nail every movement of the Holy Spirit. It is the principle that matters: the fashioning of our worship, and of our lives, according to the Mind of Christ. Numbers are of little account with God; our Lord said, not "When two or three thousand," nor "When two or three hundred," but "When two or three are gathered together in *My Name*, there am I in the midst of them." Let us aim at getting things right at the centre. A small company, worshipping and communicating together in the spirit of humility and love and fellowship, may be better pleasing to God than a full cathedral. We need to ponder much on the Church as the Body of Christ, and on the thought of ourselves as "a worshipping body" rather than as "a body of worshippers." [1]

At a time when we are being "recalled to religion" the Church must bid men come to Christ Himself in true faith and repentance; and, in leading them back to corporate worship, must see that this worship is in true lineal descent from His act in the Upper Room, when He said, "Do this in remembrance of Me," "Take, eat," "Drink ye all of this."

[1] Cf. *The Parish Communion*, pp. 18, 307.

At the close of a parochial mission people often put up a " memorial of the mission "; and this memorial, whether it be of stone, metal or wood, in time wears out. In giving us the Holy Eucharist, Jesus Christ gave us a living memorial of His mission, of His life and death and resurrection, until His coming again. He was sending out His Apostles to bear witness to Him to the ends of the earth; He knew they could only do this if they kept in closest union with the Father and in closest fellowship with one another, in the power of the Spirit; and here was the means—" Go on doing this, as My Memorial."

Parish priests bear witness to the binding and holding power of the Parish Communion and breakfast, in times when, through sickness or from other causes, they have been obliged to be away from their flocks. Certainly it is very evident that apart from blessing to *individuals*, the lasting effect of a Mission is far greater when the existing life is consolidated, and the new life incorporated, into the Parish Communion.

This leads me to speak of the introduction of the Parish Eucharist in a parish. One of the writers in *The Parish Communion* speaks of " a year's preparation and teaching." [1]

This is, I am sure, necessary and good if the change is to be made (so to speak) in cold blood, especially where there has been a long and settled tradition of another kind. I should like, however, to bear witness to the way in which the Holy Spirit sometimes brings this new order into being as part of the spiritual

[1] Cf. *The Parish Communion*, p. 181. Others testify to the value of the Liturgical Mission. See *Parish Communion*, pp. 249–53.

rebirth of a parish in a mission. It can happen thus:
The missioner asks that on the Sundays of the mission
the communicants will make, so far as possible, one
great act of worship and intercession and communion
together as the Family of God; and he may say that
he and the other missioners would greatly value the
opportunity of meeting their fellow-communicants
at a simple breakfast afterwards. The close of breakfast gives an informal opportunity of saying a little
more about the principle of Christian fellowship; and
as the mission goes forward, the idea lays hold of the
minds and affections of the people, so that, at the end
of the mission, it has often come to pass that they want
it to continue.

Here I would add two cautions, based on experience.
First, the suggestion is likely to be made that the
breakfast should be held once a month. I would reply
that a small parish breakfast weekly is better than a
larger one monthly; a monthly breakfast tends to fix in
people's minds a monthly Communion as the standard.
But the regular weekly act of worship, Communion,
and family-fellowship, even if the numbers be smaller,
is worth more than the inflated Communions at the
Festivals.

Secondly, in most parishes it is necessary to provide
an earlier Celebration for those who cannot come at
9. I would strongly advise that it should be put
earlier than the accustomed hour of 8, even if it
be only a quarter of an hour earlier; otherwise the
force of habit proves too strong, and people gravitate
to the old time.

In introducing the Parish Communion and Parish
breakfast, it is very important that all Christian

tenderness and consideration should be shown to those who have been accustomed all their lives to worship in a different way; especially in country places, where people move slowly, and where the parish church is the only church within easy reach, and is the church of the village, the church for all sorts and conditions of men. When introducing better ways of worship, it is unnecessary and unchristian to decry ways of worship that are less good; there must be serious defects in the person who " cannot worship " or " cannot find God " at Sung Mattins or Sung Mass. At the same time, while showing all consideration for the older people, it is the priest's duty to take long views, and think what is best for the building-up of the Church family over a stretch of ten or twenty years or more.

Of course it goes without saying that every parish is " *the* most difficult parish in Christendom."

The vicar in a poor London parish, when asked by a missioner whether he would allow a 9 o'clock Eucharist and breakfast during a Mission, wrote a letter (it afterwards became classical) in which he gave seventeen reasons why the idea, though a beautiful one, would not work in his parish. The missioner hard-heartedly turned down all seventeen reasons, and said, " Give it a chance." The vicar made an act of faith, and accepted the proposal. Afterwards he could not thank God enough that he had done so, and at the time of his death (fifteen years later) three leading parishioners who had been most opposed to the change being made, wrote to the Bishop begging that, whoever might be appointed, the 9 o'clock Eucharist and breakfast might be maintained.

The Parish Communion is surely the way that has
been given us whereby people of the Evangelical and
of the Catholic traditions may meet and communicate
together and sit down afterwards to breakfast, without
distressing each other, and with great mutual benefit.
It is of the highest importance that the Parish Communion should not become the badge or property of
any party; it should be the way of transcending
parties, and of meeting " in Christ."[1]   A missioner
lately found himself in a parish where there was
Benediction, and everything as on the " Western
Front," and here the Parish Eucharist and breakfast
were most strongly established.   Within a fortnight
he found himself, with another missioner, taking a
mission in a parish where there was not a candle on the
altar.   The parish priest had sometimes been unable
to celebrate at 8 because there was no one present,
and the principal Communion had been at 6.30 p.m.
The missioners were given full leave to preach what they
believed.   Some of the people, including the vicar,
made their first Confession; and a nine o'clock

[1] The Vicar of S. George's, Battersea, representing the
Evangelical Tradition, writes, " This is a very poor slum Parish,
which two and a half years ago had Mattins at 11 a.m. (congregation varied between 4 and 8—8 on a good day!) Holy Communion at 8.15 a.m. consisted of about the same numbers. We
now have only one service in the morning, and the numbers
vary between 20 and 30. . . . I strongly believe the Holy Communion should be the central act of worship—it is essentially
an Evangelical Service."

From S. Saviour's, Poplar (Fr. Dolling's old Church), comes an
account of High Mass every Sunday at 8 o'clock, followed by
breakfast. This was begun nearly forty years ago by Bishop
Trollope.

The present vicar writes : " In my early days, we were delighted
if the numbers of communionists at the 8 a.m. Mass reached 50 ;
now we are disappointed with anything under 200."

Eucharist, quite plain, but with four hymns, and followed by breakfast, was begun and continued with great conviction and enthusiasm. The missioners did not occupy themselves with externals, but simply tried to preach Christ and lead people to Him in the sacramental ways of His appointment. The hunger for Christ and for a direct and simple worship, which undoubtedly exists in many hearts, must not be turned down as something foreign to the Catholic Faith or alien to the Gospel.

Next I desire to mention a point which the parish priests who wrote the papers in this book will naturally suppress. It cannot be the ideal thing that Sunday, the high feast of Christians, should be the weekly *fast* for so many good priests. It is the day on which they do much of their hardest work. They are indeed glad to offer that fast till mid-day out of love for Christ and for their people, but for many men it is a great strain; bad for work, and bad for health. If the service is over by 10 o'clock or soon after, they can then breakfast with their people, and be ready to take whatever services may be at a later hour. There is a use also to be made of the later hours of Sunday morning, both by clergy and some of the laity: for the teaching of the children; perhaps in some places for serious and systematic preaching and teaching;[1] or for street evangelism.

It will be noticed that the writers of these papers vary considerably in their estimate of the value and necessity of the fast before Communion.

In this, as in other matters, each has been left free to

[1] See Bishop Karney's suggestion, in *An Ambassador in Chains* (Mowbray, 1937, p. xi).

state his own convictions. The Editor is not respon-sible for the views of the contributors, neither are the contributors responsible for the Editor's views.

But about one thing probably all would be agreed: that the stress must constantly be laid upon that of which the fast is but an outward expression—namely, the preparation of the soul; faith and repentance towards God, and to be in love and charity with all men.

No outward increase of numbers can please God where these conditions are absent, and we must see to it that the stress upon the outward preparation of fasting is not more prominent than the stress upon the inward preparation of the soul. Otherwise we shall be in danger of cleansing the outside of the cup and leaving the inside abominable.

It is *reality* in our life and in our worship that God looks for: " For such the Father seeketh to be His worshippers."

Parish priests who are leading their people to worship Sunday by Sunday at the Parish Eucharist, in which Offering and Communion are united, will need to weigh in their minds, that they are thereby bringing people to face the claim of Christ on the *whole* of their life.

It may be possible " to hear Mass " or to " attend Mattins " without facing this issue. We have " been to church," and that may be all.

But where the majority are communicating, we cannot escape the thought, " Am I ready to receive Christ? "—" Am I living the life of abiding in Him? "

Yet is not this just as it should be? It may sift out our congregation, but it will increase its reality. This, along with the proper requirements for the

administration of Holy Baptism and Confirmation,[1] will
do much to purify the Church from that nominal
Christianity which we all feel to be utterly alien to Him
" whose eyes are as a flame of fire, and out of Whose
mouth proceedeth a sharp two-edged sword."

A glance at the list of testimonies will show that they
are fairly representative: town and country and new
areas in England, Scotland and Wales, South Africa,
Australia and India have all borne their witness.

To many, the paper from the vast evangelical parish
in Newcastle (Ch. 2) will have special interest, showing
how the Parish Communion is helping to hold together
the newly confirmed, and stablish them in loyalty to
Christ and His Church.

I have thought it best that each of us should use, in
writing, the terms we are accustomed to, as being most
natural, trusting that no one will find reason for offence
at this.

The paper at the end, by Fr. Hebert, is different in
character from the others, but without it the book
would have fallen short of usefulness. It also forms
a link with his larger book *The Parish Communion*.

The letter and paper of suggestions have both been
in actual use in a parish. (Appendix 3, 4.)

The final word is from a voice now silent through long
sickness: I could not forbear including it out of
reverent affection for the writer—Fr. Waggett.

It is impossible to thank by name all the many
people who by their advice, typing, and writings have
made this book possible; but, in addition to the
contributors, I should like to thank Bishop Gwynne
of Egypt and the Sudan, who writes in warm support

[1] See p. 125.

of the general purpose of the book, and tells of the Sunday morning breakfasts after Holy Communion at Khartoum: " Officers, non-commissioned officers, and privates, as well as men and women of the civil community breakfasting together." They have, too, a Sunday Evening Supper Club. " The Patriarch of the Orthodox Church, Meletios, coming to one of our evening services in the Cathedral . . . noticed our white table-cloths all laid ready for the supper, and asked what it meant. I told him it was a supper for those who had been attending the church. He asked whether they were holy people who came, to which I responded that few of them would call themselves ' holy,' but I was pleased to think that the great majority were guided and influenced by the Holy Spirit, and so were saints in that sense. He promptly observed, ' This is an agape.' "

The mention of " table-cloths " prompts a reference to a custom which at least illustrates the new " family spirit " which the Holy Spirit is creating among us. At Oakworth (Yorks) those who form the Sunday breakfast-party have their names embroidered on the table-cloth; and when one of the family dies, a cross is put with the name. Down the middle of the cloth are these words, " One family we dwell in Him."

Secondly, I would thank the Dean of S. Albans for notes on the 9.30 Eucharist and (stand-up) breakfast at the Cathedral. Here, those who intend to communicate, each place a wafer in a ciborium as a means of developing the true meaning of the offertory—the people's offering.[1]

---

[1] Essay i, p. 7. See also, H. de Candole, *The Church's Offering*, Ch. IV (Mowbray, 1s. 6d.), and the teaching, along with words

Thirdly, Fr. de Candole, Liturgical Missioner of the Diocese of Chichester, for help and advice, especially on a point hardly mentioned in the papers —the part of a leader, or conductor of devotions, kneeling amongst the people, an office in early days fulfilled by the deacon.[1]

Lastly, Dr. Lowther Clarke, the Editorial Secretary of S.P.C.K., without whose help and encouragement this little book could not have been written.

As I have read and re-read the papers, two things seem to stand right out.

(1) The *root of the movement is principle*. Each man has had a vision. He has asked God to show him how to work out the principle in his parish. And, often unconscious that others were doing the same thing, has been led to the same conclusion as they. The Holy Spirit " maketh men to be of one mind in an house."

(2) The *fruit is joy*. One writer after another has testified to the joyfulness of the worship and of the breakfast, notably in papers 1, 8 and 9 (which I had almost headed " Now Magdalen hath left her moan and cheerfully doth sing ").

" The fruit of the Spirit is joy." When the Holy Spirit descended at Pentecost " They did eat their meat with gladness, and singleness of heart." " Make Thy chosen people joyful."

---

of great wisdom on the Communion for simple People, at the end of the Church Army Hymn Book.

[1] A strong witness to the value of the leader has come from Al c Macdonald, Vicar of Tonge Moor, Bolton, Lancs; and a description from St. John's, Newcastle, will be found in *The Parish Communion*, Ch. XIII, pp. 274–79, now published in smaller form.

B

And *the issue*. " Ite, Missa est " are the final words said to millions of Christians at the end of every Mass. Link these words on to Christ's own words at the end of His Ministry: Ite—" Go ye "—into all the world, and preach the Gospel unto every creature, and lo, I am with you alway even unto the end of the world. [1]

Here is the true purpose of the Eucharist. It is a means, not an end; a beginning, not a finish. We have worshipped together, as Christ's Body, we have pleaded His Sacrifice, we have received His life. What for?

To go out into the streets around, into the houses, into the factories and offices, to show Him Whom we have received. To live Christ—to speak of Christ to others.

Unless we think of the Church as the Body of Christ, the Missionary Society filled with His Spirit to make Him known, by life and word, we shall utterly fail Him. Living, we shall die.

If we come to church just for our own special needs, or because we like the worship, or the ceremonial, or the music, or the fellowship, or the priest, we may be idolaters—putting something or somebody before Christ—loving our life, we shall lose it.

Christ's Body was born to be broken for the souls of men. " This is My Body, which is broken for you. This is My Blood, which is shed for you."

If we forget ourselves, and make our Eucharist the missionary centre of the missionary body, losing ourselves, we shall live, and dying we shall give life.

Some of us live under the conviction that " the time

[1] I owe this thought to the Vicar of Flimwell, Essay 10, p. 122. See also *Parish Communion*, p. 247, note 1.

is short." We see two movements going on side by side: the great anti-Christ movement among the nations, and at the same time a great quickening of the Spirit within the Church, leading to the purification of her worship and life, and a growing desire to witness for Christ. Soon, we believe, the clash will come, as it has already begun to come on the continent; nation will rise against nation, and kingdom against kingdom; amongst those who are called Christians, apostasy will increase; and then, in the midst, Christ will come for His own, as He foretold.[1] He told us we were not to know the day nor the hour; but we would be able to discern the signs of His coming, and we must watch and be ready. He did not lead us to expect that His Church would succeed in converting the world in this present age; rather, He said, the world, at His return, would be as in the days of Noe, or in the condition of Sodom and Gomorrah. What He did lay upon His Church was the command to *bear witness*: " This Gospel of the Kingdom shall be preached *for a testimony* to the nations, and *then* shall the end come." The result of faithful witness is more likely to be persecution and rejection than acceptance, but the witness must be borne.

The Church is the Body of Christ, and the world will treat His Mystical Body as it treated His Incarnate Body; the Church must pass through a passion, as her Master did.

And as life came to Him, after the Passion, through the Resurrection, so after the Church's passion, life will come through Christ's coming for His faithful

[1] See *The Bible Comes Alive*, by Sir Charles Marston (Eyre and Spottiswoode, 1937), conclusion.

suffering Church, when those who are " in Christ "
will be " caught up to meet Him in the air " and
" His reign on earth begin."

All this has the closest bearing on the Blessed
Eucharist. St. Paul says, " As oft as ye eat this Bread
and drink this Cup, ye do show the Lord's death, till
He come " ; and our Consecration Prayer speaks of " a
perpetual memory of that His precious death, until His
Coming again." We are warned in the Epistle to the
Hebrews " not to forsake the assembling of ourselves
together . . . and *so much the more, as ye see the day
approaching*."

Between the First Coming of our Saviour Jesus Christ,
to Bethlehem, and His Second Coming, to Olivet, there
stretches a golden chain of " comings", and each
Eucharist is a link in the chain. Those who " love
His appearing " in the Blessed Sacrament, and with
penitence and faith towards God and with love and
charity to one another welcome and receive Him at the
altar, are preparing to meet Him when He comes
again.

It was on the eve of His Passion, "in the same night
that He was betrayed," that our Master gave us this
Sacrament. May it not be that now, on the eve of His
Church's passion, He is calling us to have our feet
washed in humility and penitence, giving us again His
new commandment, " Love one another," and calling
us anew to the Sacrament of His love?

CONTENTS

NEW LIFE IN AN INDUSTRIAL PARISH

By J. W. Stratton

A Contrast

It is an ordinary Sunday morning five or six years ago in a daughter church of a large parish in an industrial town in the Home Counties. We are present at the early service at 7.30, and about fifteen to twenty people have thought it worth while to begin the week by coming to receive the Bread of Life, or, if it happens to be the first Sunday in the month, there may be about double that number present at 8 o'clock.

We leave the church after the service, probably without exchanging a word with any of the other communicants, and after breakfast we return at 10 o'clock to the sung Eucharist. This is the chief, and only other, service on Sunday morning. It is sung very reverently and devoutly, and obviously means much to those present. The congregation consists of about seventy children, who behave extremely well, but there are not more than twenty other people besides. Some of these were present at the early service, but most of them have not received the Holy Communion (unless it is the first Sunday in the month), nor do they intend to do so, and this in spite of the fact that during the service prayers are said and hymns sung in which it is assumed that one of the great objects of the service is to give the sacred Food of Christ's Body and Blood to the faithful.   Two, three, or at the most, four, elderly people approach the altar at the communion time.

Now let us return to the present and visit the same church on any ordinary Sunday of this year 1938. The early service, held always now at 7.30, remains unchanged in character, and although the faces have changed somewhat, there is no change in the average number of communicants who attend it—a fact which, in view of what is to follow, is deserving of comment. But instead of the old 10 o'clock Children's Eucharist— for such it was—there is now a Parish Communion at 9. The children are still there in the same numbers, but beside these there are numbers of young men and maidens, men and women also of middle age, a few nearing the end of their allotted span and, perhaps best of all, husbands and wives with their young children, some of them only infants in arms.   When the com- munion time comes, first the servers are communicated and then almost the entire congregation, with the exception of the children.   On most Sundays there are seventy to seventy-five communicants, at great festivals nearly 100, and never, even on the worst Sundays in winter or in the middle of the summer holidays, less than fifty.   This, with seventy or more children and some of the communicants from the early service who return at 9, in a church accommodating only 200, means that on every Sunday morning the church is nearly full.   Such is the change which the 9 o'clock

Eucharist has made in this district, or rather the change which would be most obvious to a stranger who visited the church five or six years ago and returned to-day.

How it Came About

It happened as the result of a mission held in the spring of 1933, when the 9 o'clock Eucharist, followed by a breakfast, was tried as an experiment. Towards the end of the mission a meeting of the Church Council and other regular communicants was called to consider the advisability of making the change. The reasons for it were explained and people were asked to express their views. Some said one thing and some said another, and a vote, if it had been taken, would almost certainly have been 50 : 50. Therefore no vote was taken, but the parish priest announced his decision to continue the experiment for six months, and then to call another meeting to review the situation.

The next Sunday was Easter day, and need not be considered, but on Low Sunday, when the new arrangement really began, there were fifty-five communicants at 9 o'clock. There were also ten communicants at the early service, making a total for the day of sixty-five. The previous Low Sunday total was twenty-four. Numbers did not, however, remain quite at this level. During the six months experimental period the average number of communicants at 9 o'clock was forty-five, and at the early service nineteen. The average per Sunday was therefore sixty-four whereas for a number of years previous to the change the average number of communicants per Sunday, including the first Sunday in the month and festivals, had been only twenty-seven.

During the six months experimental period instructions were given on the meaning of the Parish Communion, and at the end of the period we met again to take stock of the situation. The increase in numbers was incontrovertible, many found the new order of things a very convenient one for personal or domestic reasons, and a number of people now felt that the change ought to be permanent. Many, on the other hand, felt misgivings and gave utterance to them. The more serious objections were on such questions as the effect on the attendance of the children, the question of fasting communion, the disturbance to individual devotion caused by the large number of communicants going to and from the altar, and the strange objection that the breakfast was a bribe to people to come to church.

These objections were listened to, explanations and assurances were given, and there was ample opportunity for discussion. Again no vote on the question was taken. It would probably still have resulted in only a narrow majority in favour of the change, and might have accentuated differences. Instead the parish priest stressed very strongly that, although the change had in many ways its practical advantages, it was, far more, a matter of principle. He said that for the past twelve years it had become more and more his conviction that a Eucharist at which the majority of those present did not communicate was something less than the service which our Lord instituted, and that the act of communion ought not to be separated from the offering of " our sacrifice of praise and thanksgiving." He said that, if this principle was a true one, it ought to be adopted, and that its results were bound, in the long run, to be beneficial. He therefore announced his decision to continue the 9 o'clock Eucharist until further experience might seem to make another review of the situation desirable.[1]

That further review has never yet become necessary. The change has been justified in its results, and ever since there has been a gradual increase and building up in numbers and, still more, in the Christian spirit of love, joy and fellowship one with another. Monthly communicants have become weekly communicants, lapsed communicants have returned, whole families now come to the Lord's own service together, the newly confirmed become more securely established, and new people are continually being drawn into the fellowship which radiates from our altar. The first Sunday in the month is no longer " Communion Sunday "; Communion Sunday is every Sunday, and the number of communions made each Sunday is now more than three times as many as on any average Sunday before the change was made.

The Service Outlined

Except that the service is now, in the proper sense, a Communion, it continues very much on the old lines. Vestments are worn, there is one chief server or clerk (who wears a tunicle), and also two servers, who carry lights. On festivals incense is also used and there is a procession. The singing is congregational and hearty rather than talented. The music is Merbecke. We begin with an introit hymn and take advantage

---

[1] Nothing could have been done without the goodwill and support of the Rector of the parish; and this was given whole-heartedly.

of the provisions of the 1928 Prayer Book in regard to
" the Introduction." The Collect is sung with inflec-
tions, but the Epistle is read in the natural voice, facing
the people, as it is felt that the sense of the words,
sometimes very involved, can be more clearly conveyed
if the passage is read. A short hymn, or part of a
hymn, is sung as a Gradual, during which the priest,
with the clerk and the other servers with their lights
(and the incense), move slowly down to the chancel
step, where the Holy Gospel is solemnly sung, facing
the people. All sing the usual responses before and
after, and the triumphant strains of the organ continuing as the priest and servers return to the altar, form a
climax to one of the really dramatic parts of the service.

After the Creed, notices are given out and an address
of five to ten minutes, generally of a liturgical character,
is delivered from the chancel step. This is followed by
the ceremony of the Offertory. Before the service the
oblations of bread and wine are placed in readiness on
a table, called the prothesis table,[1] at the west end of
the church, where all who enter see the eucharistic
gifts. While the Offertory hymn is being sung, the
alms are collected by the sidesmen in the usual way,
and when this has been done, two other sidesmen (the
churchwardens if present) take the oblations from the
prothesis and follow the sidesmen with the alms in
procession through the congregation. At the chancel
step they are met by the two servers with lights, who
precede them to the altar rail, where the clerk receives

---

[1] The table is the size of a credence table. It is covered with a
white cloth and over it hangs a copy of Holden's picture " Remembrance." The oblations consist of a sufficient number of
breads in a ciborium and two cruets containing the wine and
water.

first the alms, then the breads and then the cruets of wine and water, and takes each in turn to the priest at the altar. All this is carried out in complete silence, and several priests, witnessing it for the first time, have remarked on its impressiveness. On festivals incense is used at this point also, in the usual way, the thurifer preceding the taperers in the procession to the altar rails.

The biddings to prayer follow and the Prayer for the Church is said in the 1928 form. The remainder of the service follows the 1662 order. After the Consecration, to which all sing the " Amen," there is a period of silence while the priest says, privately, the Prayer of Oblation, and he then begins to sing, unaccompanied, the Agnus Dei. This is taken up by everyone, and the priest makes his own communion, after which the communion of the servers and people follows immediately. No hymn or organ is allowed at this point, but all is silence. Even the children seem to catch the spirit of this solemn moment, and the silence, lasting ten or twelve minutes, is real.

After the Blessing there is one more hymn, always of a joyful, praise type, and then the priest, having already left the altar with his servers, from the west end of the church leads the people in a very short act of thanksgiving—a practice quite " unnecessary," but introduced at the people's own request. The service lasts about sixty-five minutes (seventy-five minutes on festivals), and nearly all the communicants (with their children) then go into the Institute near by for the breakfast.

The Breakfast

The breakfast is a very simple, very happy affair.
It consists of tea, rolls and butter, marmalade, fish
paste, fruit. Generally sixty to seventy are present,
but we have on occasions had 100 or more. We do
not find it necessary to know the numbers at all
accurately beforehand. If ever there is a surplus of
food, someone is always willing to purchase it. There
are four teams of helpers responsible—one for each
Sunday in the month—and each team consists of six or
eight ladies under a leader and a second. When there
is a fifth Sunday in the month, a team of men manages
very efficiently.

Everything is put ready for the breakfast, as far as
possible, on Saturday evening. On Sunday morning
the leader of the team goes into the Institute to light
the gas under the urn and to attend to one or two small
details before 9 o'clock Mass, and she leaves the church
during the last hymn; otherwise no one is in attendance
in the Institute until the breakfast actually begins.
The helpers then wait at the tables, and clear away
and wash up afterwards. No fixed charge is made,
but a receptacle is placed on each table, and into this
all put something. Everyone knows that the actual
cost is about threepence halfpenny per head, and some
give more, some less. The result is that the breakfast is
entirely self-supporting, and we just pay our way.
Only once has it been necessary to mention finance.
Anyone is welcome at the breakfast. Young people
appreciate it because it gives them fellowship together,
and so, too, with the men in a different way; mothers
appreciate it because, on this one day in the week,

they can partake of a meal they have not had to get ready, and then go home immediately after to prepare the all-important Sunday dinner, and the children of the communicants also are happy as, like the Holy Child of old, they take their place " in the company " and freely associate with their other brothers and sisters in Christ.

The Children

Of the objections brought against the 9 o'clock Eucharist at the time of the change two or three did appear to be of a formidable nature, although, in the light of experience, the fears which some entertained have proved groundless. The first objection was in regard to the children. With the change to 9 o'clock the attendance of the children at the Eucharist did at first drop about 30 per cent. Some of the mothers, not being church-goers themselves, said that they could not get their children ready by 9 o'clock. There was a morning Sunday School at 11 and Catechism at 2.30, and they considered this was quite enough.

This did appear to be serious, especially as the parish priest believed that the theory used to justify the 10 o'clock arrangement, which had been tried for twenty years, would be far more likely to produce fruit if applied to the 9 o'clock Eucharist. The theory was that the children who attended the Eucharist regularly would become the communicants of the future, and the parish priest believed that this was far more likely to happen if the service which they attended was one at which they saw the majority of their elders actually communicating.

Again the appeal was made to principles,[1] and the matter was dealt with in this way. The 11 o'clock morning Sunday School was dropped, the Catechism was changed into a graded afternoon Sunday School, absentees were diligently looked up, the reasons for the change in the time of the service were explained to any parents who would listen sympathetically, and renewed teaching given in regard to attendance at the Eucharist. At once the tide turned, and the attendance of the children at 9 o'clock returned to the seventy average of the old days, and has continued so now for three and a half years.

Marks and stamps are given for attendance at the Eucharist, and those who do not come with their parents are encouraged to occupy the front places in church, where their teachers also are present with them. But no attempt is made to regiment the children, and the teachers are present with them simply to assist them in finding their places [2] and to set them an example of reverent and attentive worship.

Whenever possible children are encouraged to remain with their parents, if they are present, and mention must be made of the very young children (some of them babies in arms) brought with their fathers and mothers in this way. Everything is done to encourage Mr. and Mrs. Allwork to come with their family, and to revive the lost habit of family worship. There are always some half-dozen or so little ones of less than

[1] The writer desires to acknowledge his indebtedness to the series of articles on " Sunday Morning and the Children " in *Theology* for January 1927, also to the Rev. A. R. Browne-Wilkinson's *The Confirmation School* (S.P.C.K.).

[2] Each child who attends regularly has his or her own copy of *Adoremus* (S.P.C.K., 6d.).

school age—some only a few months old—present with their parents. These little ones do, naturally, at first utter somewhat inarticulate, even unorthodox praises, but they very quickly grow into the atmosphere of the worship. They do, in fact, cause very little disturbance, and when the time for communion comes, it is quite possible for Mr. Allwork to hold the baby while Mrs. Allwork goes up to the altar rail among the first batch of communicants, and then, on her return, to hand the baby back to her in time to go up himself among the last batch.

Other communicants quickly get used to this kind of thing, and do not notice it happening. If Michael Allwork, aged three, occasionally sings " Holy, Holy " at the time of Consecration, that is surely excusable, while such inaccuracies as Eileen Allwork, aged five, joining in and singing " Merry God of merry God " or " Hosanna in the High Street," are probably noticed only by Mrs. Allwork herself and Eileen's own guardian angel. If these things are thought of as detracting from the worship, there is yet another side. The value of it all to a child who, from its earliest years, grows up in the atmosphere of the Church's worship, and has, too, the example of father and mother before its eyes, is surely inestimable and can never be lost.

This also leads on to one last point about the children. Of much greater importance than the mere numbers who attend the service is the fact that a generation of children is now growing up accustomed to seeing the altar thronged Sunday by Sunday, and most of them long most ardently for the time when they will be confirmed and able to go to the altar too. It is the old story of practice being more than precept, and we

do find far more of the newly confirmed holding fast
to their communions now than was the case before.
More than 50 per cent. of those confirmed since the
change was made are still regular communicants—
most of them weekly communicants—and this, when
removals, etc., are allowed for, would seem to be
decidedly good.

Fasting Communion

The writer rigidly adheres to the rule of fasting
communion himself, believes in it as a godly discipline
of the Church, and teaches others to practise it. But
one objection urged very strongly against our 9 o'clock
Mass was that many were not fasting. Inquiry proved
that there had been much exaggeration in regard to
this matter, and that people did not, except in a very
few cases, find any greater difficulty in fasting till after
the 9 o'clock service than they did in fasting till after
the 7.30. It is also found on inquiry among Confirmation candidates that many of these, while still uncon-
firmed, do in fact come at 9 o'clock fasting, for the very
good reason that when they leave home the family has
not begun to think of breakfast, but they are just
settling down to it when these young adventurers
return soon after 10. For the communicants themselves, the breakfast after the service is a powerful aid
both in inculcating and upholding the habit of fasting
communion, and sermons on the reasons for and the
value of the practice have produced encouraging
results.

It must be mentioned that when inquiries were made
about this question, some, who had been in the habit
of communicating in the old days at the early service,

frankly admitted that they had not done so fasting. Certainly some people whose habit it is to take an early morning cup of tea on every other day do not find it at all easy to dispense with this when coming to communion. Some, in fact, had not regarded this as a breaking of their fast. However, every opportunity is taken to encourage people who find any difficulty in fasting to consult their parish priest, and not to excuse themselves, and the writer believes that at the present time almost all of the communicants at 9 o'clock come fasting. He has formed the opinion that if there are any who, after receiving teaching and instruction, do not try to fast for a 9 o'clock Communion, they would not be fasting even if they came at an earlier hour. The question, therefore, seems to be whether a devout non-fasting communion is less pleasing to our Lord than no communion at all, and it would seem that our Lord's teaching in Matt. 15. 10–20 and St. Paul's teaching in Rom. 14 have some bearing on this question. If fasting communion is reasonably possible at 9 o'clock (and it certainly is), and if the Church's rule is made clear, has the parish priest any further responsibility in the matter?

Conclusion

Other objections to the change we made arose from the contrast between a quiet early morning service, with its very individualistic atmosphere, and the corporate nature of our present sung Eucharist. Those who feel the force of this kind of objection are mostly people with the habits and point of view of a lifetime behind them, and these are naturally not easily altered or adjusted. But the answer to these objections is to be found in that " conception of the nature of the Church which appears to compel the adoption of the Parish Communion as its necessary expression in liturgy."[1]

This essay has dwelt very largely on the numerical gains resulting from the adoption of the Parish Communion in our particular case, but of far greater importance has been the growth among us of an understanding of the nature of the Church and of membership in it. Fellowship has been one of the most obvious fruits. A people, naturally somewhat clannish, has learned to open its arms and welcome into its embrace newcomers from Wales, the Tyne and the Tees, from Lancashire, Yorkshire and the West Country, and all these, with their lovely intonations, are at home in the one " family " gathering around the altar in church and afterwards at the breakfast. There is, too, a joyousness about our worship and our fellowship together which is most marked. Any two members of " the family " meeting one another during the week will invariably part with the words " Goodbye; see you on Sunday " on their lips, and on Christmas day we all bring little Christmas gifts for one another, and exchange them at the crib as we are leaving the church. Everyone is glad to " go unto the house of the Lord."

Again, there is no room for defeatism in our parochial life, but we have, through our Parish Communion, gained an outlook of abounding hopefulness, and also a new sense of corporate loyalty which has fitted us to weather the storms which must sometimes

[1] Fr. Hebert, *The Parish Communion*, p. vii.

arise. There is, too, a really missionary-hearted
enthusiasm to win others and to bring them in. So, by
God's goodness and God's grace, we are learning to
" grow up in all things unto Him, which is the head,
even Christ; from whom all the body, fitly framed and
knit together through that which every joint supplieth,
according to the working in due measure of each several
part, maketh the increase of the body unto the building
up of itself in love."

2

AN EVANGELICAL WITNESS FROM THE NORTH

By F. Baker

The parish of Byker is the east-end parish of the city of Newcastle-upon-Tyne. It is " east end " in every respect—poor, crowded and overwhelming in its difficulties and problems. It is one of the large parishes of the Church, there being more then 30,000 souls within its boundaries. There is a fairly strong Roman Catholic following, but very little Nonconformity. The parish is too poor to provide the necessary support for Nonconformist Chapels. Thus, apart from those definitely attached to the Roman Catholic Church, the whole responsibility of ministering to the souls of this immense population falls upon the Church. It is an overwhelming task, and if one allowed the weight of responsibility to press too heavily upon one's mind and conscience, one would shrink from even attempting to face the problem. There is, however, much to encourage, for although many thousands are altogether outside any form of the organisation of the Christian Church, and live their lives in forgetfulness of God, yet many hundreds, both young and old, love their Church and its message of hope. I do not speak of the deep

16

depression of this district due to long unemployment, and the hardship suffered by the whole of Tyneside is well known to the country. Sufficient to say that the work of the Church is made more difficult among people who are suffering from an enforced idleness against which they rebel. A bitterness against circumstances or fate or society as constituted does not help people to draw near to God.

This parish is Evangelical in practice and tradition, and we remain loyal to that tradition. We receive grants from the Church Pastoral Aid Society for the maintenance of the staff, and such grants are given only to Evangelical parishes. Our church, therefore, and all the services held in it are " plain," and keep as near as possible to the Evangelical interpretation of the 1662 Prayer Book. But do not imagine that our church is ugly and our worship dull. The church is very beautiful (we have just spent £7000 upon enlarging and improving it), and our services are bright and devotional. Naturally the priestly and sacramental aspect of the Christian Faith is not in keeping with our tradition.

I intend now to give you a simple and truthful account of the origin of our " Family Communion Service," telling you of its history and the position it occupies in our worship. Forgive me if I appear to be personal. As I introduced it, I cannot help but speak of it from the angle of the first person.

When I came to this parish some twelve years ago, one of my first duties was to prepare some 120 persons for the service of Confirmation. They were mostly young, the average age being sixteen years. We do not encourage persons under that age to be confirmed.

For three months we enjoyed together a time of real spiritual blessing as we sought to know more fully the will of God and the call of Jesus Christ. It is no exaggeration to say that one of the fundamental weaknesses of the Church is the loss sustained soon after Confirmation. I am told that nine out of every ten confirmed lapse from Church membership soon after they are confirmed. There are multitudes of men and women in our country who early in life gave their lives to God at their Confirmation, and yet have drifted away from God and the Church in the passing of the years. The Church of this land would be revolutionised if she could reclaim to loyal and devoted service those who have been confirmed. This was the thought constantly in my mind during the time I was preparing for Confirmation this body of young people. Would they remain faithful, or would they in time join that large body of men and women who were once so full of hope but are now the sheer dead weight of the Christian Church of our land? No person who has had the responsibility of preparing for Confirmation any body of people can avoid wondering what is to be the permanent devotion of those who sit there. Very few churches in the country would be large enough to accommodate the worshippers if all, or even most of those in that parish who had been confirmed had remained loyal to their Lord and dedicated to the service of His Church.

How, then, could I hold this body of young people for God and the service of Jesus Christ? This was constantly in my mind. Now, one feeling inevitably develops during the time of preparation. It is the feeling of fellowship with one another. At no time does the priest get so near to the hearts of his people and at no time is the sense of fellowship so strong among Christians. To be confirmed together is a bond of unity which is not common in life. It is clearly the work of the Holy Spirit. I therefore resolved that as we had been together during the time of preparation, so we should be together in our communicant life, and I gradually made this a part of my definite teaching. It is an aspect of Confirmation and Communion which needs greater stressing in these days. We live, even in our Christian life, far too much as separated units. Yet this is entirely foreign to the meaning of the Church, and clearly foreign to the whole meaning of the Holy Communion. To meet this felt need I arranged that those who were confirmed together should come to their first Communion together as one body at 9 a.m. on Christmas Day. It was to be an additional Communion Service for them, although, of course, it could not be limited to them. Thus our " Family Communion Service " was instituted, and from that day to this has increasingly shown itself to be a service of worship and fellowship for the whole parish.

Most of you will know that the morning services of any industrial parish have of recent years been very sparsely attended. The poor people, on the whole, reserve their worship of God until the evening. Their mornings are spent in household duties or in idleness. There are many, many, churches in which you will find a large body of worshippers at Evensong, while the church has been almost empty for the morning services. To teach people to worship God in the morning is one of the results of the Family Communion Service.

Sunday by Sunday at 9 a.m. a body of people come to offer their worship at this service, and so give God the first thought of the day. The whole of the day is influenced by this worship offered to God in the morning. I venture to affirm that the spiritual life of the parish is really deeply affected by the " morning watch."

Again, one real problem in parishes of this type is the training of leaders in Sunday School and general parish organisation. Naturally we here, in such a parish, have very large Sunday Schools, and require a large number of teachers. Many such parishes find that the supply of teachers is the chief difficulty of Sunday School work. I have found that the 9 a.m. service simplifies the provision of such teachers, and also gives them a greater value and effectiveness. At this service, as at no other, it is possible to build up a body of devoted young people and to give them training in doctrine and history. Most ordinary sermons are hortatory; at the " Family Communion Service " the emphasis ought to be devotional and instructive. Most of the Sunday School teachers attached to this parish are generally present Sunday by Sunday at 9 a.m., and I know that their work is all the better for their presence. Out of this service it is possible to build up a strong body of people who are really devoted to our Lord and to His service. They become leaders because they hear His call, and thus are ready to serve Him. Leadership depends ultimately upon devotion, and not upon education or ability. Most Sunday School teachers who make their first appearance of the day before the class they are to teach without having spent some time with God are not giving God their best service, nor are they really fully helping the children.

It might be well now if I tried to set before you the type of service in which we share. You will remember that we are an Evangelical parish, and that our practice and teaching are loyal to this interpretation of the Gospel. There is therefore no adornment of this service such as you would expect to find in other churches. But we endeavour to bring music and brightness into the service so that a complete act of worship may be offered. We commence with a hymn, carefully chosen, either to accord with the season of the Church's year or some other aspect of prayer or thanksgiving which seems appropriate to the day and the time of the day. The Communion Service as set in our Book of Common Prayer is then faithfully followed. The Kyrie is sung to a simple setting which everyone knows. Every effort is used to make the service congregational in character. At the place appointed in the Prayer Book an address is given— short, with an emphasis laid upon teaching, and not on appeal. There is then the hymn during the taking of the Offertory, and the service follows as written to the Prayer of Consecration. A suitable hymn is then sung by all, and the administration takes place. Reverence is in the heart of us all, and this act of Communion on the part of a large body of young people is one of the deepest spiritual experiences of all our worship. There is no non-communicating attendance. After the administration the service follows the Prayer Book, and as a Recessional we sing either a suitable hymn or the Nunc Dimittis. The whole service lasts one hour. So the young people are free for the rest of the morning to enjoy a walk or to spend their time at home. When they are at the factory or in shops all the week, both fresh air and home have their natural attractions.

At certain times of the year, especially during Lent, we make an effort to secure the attendance of all our communicants at this service, and I try to obtain the services of a visiting preacher to give a course of instruction. Often as many as 300 young people are in church for these services, and they present a most valuable opportunity for deepening the spiritual life and for giving definite instruction upon the Christian faith. One of our real difficulties to-day is to overcome the abysmal ignorance of most people to the very simplest elements of the Christian faith. The " teaching " of the average Council school about the Christian faith is very vague. The duty of worship is very rarely taught. This service therefore provides a golden opportunity to supply this need.

Much more could be said about this " Family Communion Service," for the problem we are all facing is to try to inculcate the duty of worship in a generation of people who seem to be drifting away from God. I would commend this method to any parish priest in such a parish as this. It will take some effort, and it will make the Sunday duty additionally heavy; but in course of time you will find your efforts repaid by a deeper devotion on the part of many of your younger people. You will be building on a solid foundation which will last through the years, for we shall continue to lament our failures until we bring our people to God. Mere organisation will not hold them in these days. Real religion must express itself in worship.

3

THE VILLAGE PROBLEM IN WALES

By R. H. Davies

The Witness of a Country Parish

ACCORDING to the *Handbook of the Church in Wales* the acreage of this parish is 5788, and the population only 668, typical, I believe, of the rural parishes in West Wales. When there are many acres and few souls, it inevitably means a long way to walk to church for the majority of our people. In the case of our bigger farmers this does not matter a great deal, as they have their cars; but only about four of my little congregation enjoyed this luxury. The majority of my people were small farmers, and in many cases the greater part of the work at home was left to the mother, while the father sought additional work elsewhere. Then, again, there were labourers, some on the farms and some picking up a job wherever it could be found. There were two villages, in one of which was the parish church, and in the other a Church school; we also had a State school. In each village there were two shops, and a " pub " in one (the only one in a parish of nearly six square miles, and even this one had to be closed through lack of patronage). The Church school was licensed for services; in another corner of the parish there was a beautiful little mission church cared for by the county family, people whose hearts were really filled with the love of God and who gave up the whole of their lives in the service of God and His Church. The parish church was down in the main village at another end of the parish. I think I can convey to your minds the idea of distance by means of the picture of an equilateral triangle, the sides three miles in length, with the parish church, the mission church, and the Church school at each corner. As there was only a Sunday School on Sunday at the Church school, my people in that part of the parish had three miles to come to church; the average distance for the others was one and a half miles, with the exception of the few villagers living around the old parish church, beautiful in spite of the ravages of restoration.

I was single-handed, so my chief difficulty is seen at once: How was I to make it reasonably possible for my people to come to Holy Communion every Sunday? There was also the problem of local tradition. For many years my people had been accustomed to Holy Communion at 8 a.m., at which there was seldom anybody assisting other than the Rectory household; the people chiefly communicated at the service held once a month after 10.30 Mattins. There was a monthly service of Holy Communion at the mission church also. Mattins and Evensong were sung every Sunday at the parish church, and Evensong every Sunday afternoon at the mission church; a sermon was delivered at each of these services. Looking back on it all now, I know there was no real Protestant spirit prevailing—due, I am sure, to the faithful services of a long line of priests, one of whom, in my mind, made the parish, and will

always live in the minds and hearts of the people. I
did, however, find my people shy of the word " Catholic," and the monthly service of Holy Communion,
which was the only one fairly well attended, did not
possess that atmosphere of reverence which suggests a
body of men and women who had come to meet their
Lord to worship Him and give Him thanks. This was
probably the reason why I found myself up against
another big difficulty; many saw very little difference
between Church and Chapel. The Anniversary Services at the local chapel, which are the " great festivals "
of our dissenting brethren, meant for me almost an
empty church; while the chapel used to close down
the night of our Harvest Thanksgiving, and we had
an over-full church. This mutual admiration was,
after all, only skin-deep. Somewhere back about
1905 there had arisen a bitter feud between the then
rector, who was at that time made a Bishop, and the
dissenting brethren led by the local minister, known,
I believe, as the " Black Bishop." Any little accidental
circumstance could easily awaken this dozing dog,
and then there would follow a period of anything but
mutual admiration.

This latter domestic trouble may appear irrelevant
to my subject, but I mention it because it was a very
real part of the atmosphere in which I was put to
work. At the time I could see no clear path, but I
brought with me from my previous curacy one treasure
of truth taught me by the example and kindly counsel
of two wonderful vicars: my people must be guided
to love our Lord at all times, and especially in the
Blessed Sacrament of the Altar. At that time Fr.
Hebert had not published his *Liturgy and Society*, and

we did not possess the witness and guidance of *The Parish Communion*; so the only thing I could do was to puzzle out for myself the best way and most convenient time for my people. It had to be made possible for the family to come together at the same time. The hour of 8 a.m. was impossible. Farmers in West Wales nowadays sell their milk, and the cans have to be out on the stands at the roadside by about 7 a.m. This is not the only work the farmer has to do, but there did seem to be a definite break in the work on Sunday after milking time. I decided on the hour of 9.30, and after I had been in the parish but a short time, I made my intention known. Had I heard and read about it as much as is possible to-day, I might not have set out on the adventure with so little preparation. In any case, I was not introducing the Parish Communion with the more detailed knowledge I have of it to-day—my object was to make it possible for the majority of my people to come to the Lord's House on the Lord's Day for the Lord's Service—nor was I then as aware of the Church as the Body of Christ; but herein, I believe, lies an important fact. I did not have in my mind more than the absolute importance of Holy Communion and the most convenient time to call my people together to " come and see "; yet it did result in bringing to us all a sense of family corporate worship which we did not possess before. The reaction to my announcement was what I expected, and the general opinion of my people can be fairly summed up in words spoken to me in the vestry after the service by my verger: " Rector," he said, " me and you will be having a nice little service on our own." I had, however, the advantage of being in a country parish; and perhaps, being bred and born in the country myself, God enabled me to find a way into the hearts of country people. All I can say is, they were prepared to listen to me when I spoke to them in their homes, and, above all, they were prepared to give it a trial, with the result that they came, and kept on coming. The mere introduction of a Parish Communion at 9.30 was not an " Open Sesame " to all the doors that were still closed, and I don't think there was any real progress until the influence of my first Confirmation class was felt. The emphasis on the bounden duty of worship at the altar did make a difference to the children, and to this day I believe they had more influence over their parents than I had. It does count for something when a girl of thirteen will get up and come to Holy Communion, leaving her parents and the rest of the household in bed.

Owing to the fact that I had two churches and had to do the work single-handed, the plan I adopted was this. When there was sung Eucharist, as we called it at first, at the parish church, there was Holy Communion at 8 a.m. at the mission church. The following Sunday the order was reversed. I also had Morning Prayer at 11 o'clock at the church where Holy Communion was at 8 a.m. This made it difficult to introduce the parish breakfast, and I did not do so. I wish now I had, as it would have been a valuable aid in leading the people to accept the importance of fasting communion. It is not easy to lead a man, or indeed for a man himself to learn, to love our Lord in the Blessed Sacrament to the degree that he will do three hours' work on an empty stomach.

D

A parish breakfast might have brought them half-way and enabled them to take just a little food, as an act of reverence to the spiritual food in Holy Communion. However, as I have not tried the experiment of a parish breakfast, I am not in a position to pass any definite opinion; what I have said is only the impression I hold now when I look back on those very happy six years.

As regards the details of the order of our 9.30 sung Eucharist, I need only add one or two points of interest. They had never, as far as anybody could remember, sung the service. To begin with, we only sang the hymns; but after Evensong on Wednesday nights we practised Merbecke's setting as in the Faith Press 1*d.* publication. I am afraid we did not always give a correct rendering of the music, and there were some alterations we made for our own convenience! We were often out of tune, but somehow or other it did not seem to matter; we were making " a joyful noise unto the Lord." Numbers, we all know, are not important; when the weather was bad, those who lived two or three miles away were not always present, although country people, with this great distance to come and no pavements, are not nearly as frightened of rain as town folk. A Londoner who was present at one service told me he had seen something that morning he had never seen before: twenty-two men of fine physique kneeling side by side before the altar. One day my verger came to me and reminded me of what he had told me, and wanted to tell me he was glad he was wrong.

Up to this point there has been no thought or mention of the word " party," and there is nothing one wishes more than to keep this movement free from any party label. Personally I am hoping and praying that we will be led by the Holy Spirit to find in this the happy combination of Catholic and Evangelical. In his book *The Beloved Community*, Canon Lloyd writes of the inevitable state of tension between the claims of the community and the freedom of the individual, and sets forth as an ideal the keeping of this tension at a creative level. Since reading it I have been wondering whether there is not the same ideal for us to aim at in our expression of worship, to keep the tension between corporate and individual, the Catholic and Evangelical, at a creative level. Those of us who are working in parishes such as the one I am writing about, have perhaps to face a peculiar difficulty. There are many things taken for granted and regarded as the normal, especially by us priests; but we are far in advance of lay folk, especially in the districts of which I have had experience. The minimum of decency and reverence will by some be interpreted as " High Church tendencies." I was asked by a farmer in my last parish, " Why do you talk of the Catholic faith? " and then he added, " I always thought every member of the Church of England was a Protestant." In addition to this attitude, I found myself again and again accused of making people too familiar with Holy Communion. My experience was, and is to-day in my new parish, which is industrial, that I am for some time regarded with suspicion. Take, for example, the introducing of servers. This helps us to convince our people that they have a part in the service, and that it is not a case of only something done for them by the priest; yet the existence of servers, in the opinion

of many, is a sign of " party." It may be of interest
to some to know that I have since found less opposition
when, to begin with, I have used men rather than boys.
Again, the use of wafers and the wearing of vestments
will mean suspicion, though I once met a man who
thought the chasuble was a peculiar kind of hood.
Even frequent communion is, in the minds of some, a
sign of " party." In my experience this suspicion
does not last long, and to-day in my old parish I am
sure the discontinuance of my " new ideas " would
be resented.

Finally, I would like to bear witness to what the
introduction of the 9.30 Parish Communion did for my
parish. It gave to my people a deeper meaning of
Church membership. They responded in a wonderful
way to my scheme for beautifying the interior of our
church. Our Bishop came down to us one Sunday
morning and dedicated thirty-three gifts, ranging from
an oak altar, made in the parish, down to a book-
marker. It was a wonderful morning, and the service
was such as we shall never forget. It also gave to my
people a more definite faith, and put an end to at
least 80 per cent. of that sentimental kind of religion
which said " there is no difference between us, we are
all going the same way home." This had rather a
curious effect on our Chapel brethren; at first there
was definitely a gulf between us, but at the same time
we commanded their respect. Here is an incident to
illustrate what I mean. Good Friday was kept as a
holiday; in a neighbouring parish there was at one
of the chapels a " tea-fight " and Eisteddfod, one of
the most popular events of the year, to which both
Church and Chapel people went in crowds. From

my own village and district numbers were conveyed by a merchant living in the village. In response to my appeal, my people decided not to go, and as the majority of my choir were competitors, you can imagine the storm of opinion against us. The wind was taken out of the sails of the opposition when it became known that the merchant, a prominent Chapel man, had decided not to take out his conveyance, and intended coming to the church services. From that day forward Good Friday was observed in a Christian manner. When the excitement caused by my changes had died down, I can truthfully say Chapel people had a far greater respect for the Church, and we Church people had a far greater respect for the faith and sincerity of our Chapel brethren; I personally could number many of them as my friends.

It is impossible to judge exactly what place the love of our Lord has in the heart of another; but the continued loyalty of Church members, the sacrifice of time and money made again and again in response to appeals, could not have been the result of anything less than the appeal of the worship at the altar which they had learnt to love.

Like most other folk, they loved a sermon. I gave them one at 9.30, again at 11 o'clock, and also at both Evensongs; and I did try in this way to give them the best I could. We had our ups and downs; there were times when I imagined there was a falling away; but back they would come again. In addition to the Sunday services we had a daily Communion at 7.45; two or three would always come, and the farmers often told me they loved to hear the old church bell ringing when they were out in the fields. It was a happy

time, and I felt we were moving towards the ideal
when the worship at the altar would indeed be the
centre of our life.   Not long ago we took the Mothers'
Union from my present parish down to West Wales;
on our way home we were entertained to tea by the
M.U. of my old parish.   Naturally I took them into
the dear old church; and there before the altar two
who had lived in broken fellowship for a long time
spoke to one another, and were brought together again.
Was it the atmosphere of holy beauty inspired by our
9.30 Parish Communion?

4

THE EVANGELISATION OF A NEW HOUSING DISTRICT

By John Darlington

RED roofs. Rough-cast walls. Trim front gardens. New blocks of shops. A large modern school. A daily exodus to the City. Many children and few elderly people. A long, low-built Church hall. In some such words might be described the new housing districts springing up round London, as round every big town at the present time.

The writer of this essay was sent to just such a " new district " some six and a half years ago. At that time roads were still largely unmade and portions of the parish-to-be were still green fields. How could the task of building up a Christian family best be undertaken?

Actually two processes went on side by side. The task was approached from the angle of experiment on the one hand, and from that of a growing experience on the other. It thus came about that much which was done in the early days would have been done differently if it could have been done with the experience of the doing of it in possession.

What actually was done? First, the local Council school was hired from the Education Authority. Secondly, permission was obtained from the builders of the estate to use an old mansion (afterwards demolished) for the holding of services. Thirdly, Evening Prayer was announced, and duly held in the large room available there. Lastly, a Celebration of Holy Communion was provided during Sunday mornings.

The months went by, each crowded with new contacts and interests. Presently the walls of the Church hall, built through the efforts of both the diocese and the ancient parish out of which the new district was being taken, began to rise. In a few months it was completed, furnished and in due course dedicated by the diocesan in the midst of a large congregation of residents. The time had come for the establishment of regular services and organisations. What were they to be?

Despite one or two tentative experiments in the days of the old house, with something more conventional it was decided to hold the Holy Communion at 8 a.m., Morning Prayer at 11 a.m. and Evening Prayer at 6.30 p.m., with a second Celebration on certain Sundays in the month. For a time all seemed to be well. The evening service in particular was attended by a fair congregation, and the usual nucleus of the faithful, to be found in so many parishes, came to the " early service." Presently, however, the situation seemed less satisfactory. With the summer months there came an unexpected decline in the numbers present at Evening Prayer. Morning Prayer at 11 a.m. never attracted many people. The Holy Communion at 8 o'clock retained its faithful few, but there were no marked signs of increase.

What was to be done? Slowly it began to dawn on the writer that something was wrong; that there was no centre for parish life, no " hearth-fire " round which the family could be gathered. Neither Morning nor Evening Prayer, not even the Communion itself in its bare form at 8 a.m. on Sundays, provided what seemed to be needed.

Various rearrangements of service hours were tried. In particular the plan of having the Eucharist at 11 a.m., immediately following Morning Prayer at 10.30, seemed at one time to hold the solution. The desired results, however, did not follow. Those accustomed to an early Celebration continued to come at 8 o'clock. Those who worshipped at the Eucharist found a real difficulty in the practice of fasting communion. Above all, there was still lacking a real centre of unity.

So it came about that, in the fulness of time, the writer was brought to realise that there must be one great service of thanksgiving, offering and reception of communion, available for all, of whatever school of thought, a service to which all other services in some degree look, the very focus of the spiritual life of the parish.

Thus, in 1933, a scheme of worship was commenced which provided :—

(1) Morning Prayer and Litany at 8.30 a.m., in preparation for the Communion.

(2) The Parish Communion at 9 a.m., with four

hymns, music, sermon and notices; the great service of the day.

(3) At 11 a.m. a second Celebration, modelled closely on the Parish Communion, but with an instruction and catechising in place of a sermon, intended primarily for those boys and girls of eleven-plus who, for various reasons, some good and some poor, could not easily be brought to worship God in the Parish Communion two hours earlier.

(To this was added in 1935 a said Celebration at 7.30 a.m. for the benefit of those who are genuinely hindered from coming later in the day. Shortly afterwards Morning Prayer was placed at 8.15 and the Litany at 8.45.)

What was the immediate effect of this great change in the whole system of worship?

A number of new communicants appeared.

There was a large measure of loyal acceptance of the new order.

There was also a certain measure of disapproval amongst various Church people. Why had the " proper " service of Morning Prayer been taken away? Why had the " awkward hour " of nine been chosen? And so on. It was in vain that one pointed out that Morning Prayer continued to be held, and that all who wished to come could still do so. Morning Prayer without hymns at an hour other than 11 was not regarded as in any sense the same service.

But let us pass on. With the march onwards of the years, practically all the dislike of the change seems to have gone. Occasionally it is yet to be encountered, but such an attitude is, nowadays, comparatively rare.

The " Nine o'clock," as it is affectionately called, is now recognised as *the* service of the day, even by those (a small minority) who still say that they prefer the " quiet service " at half-past seven.

As for the eleven o'clock young people's Communion, it is, in the main, the boys and girls for whom it is intended who make up the congregation.

Before we pass on to some estimate of the effect of the Parish Communion upon the life of a new district, it may be interesting to give a short account of a normal Sunday morning as seen by the parish priest.

At 7.25 twelve strokes sound on the church bell.

At 7.30 the first Celebration begins. There may be a dozen or two dozen communicants.

At 8.10 twelve more strokes sound. Just two or three only at present come to Morning Prayer. Maybe more will learn to come in the future. One believes and hopes so.

At 8.40, after a quiet walk in the church garden, come twelve more strokes, and then follows the Litany so far as the words " Lord, have mercy upon us." Perhaps a dozen will be present for Litany.

In the meanwhile steps will have been heard outside, crunching the gravel path and ending either in the porch or in the passage leading to the vestry. When the doors are opened there is usually a small crowd waiting to enter.

The organist and his blower arrive. The bell rings again at 8.55, this time with twenty-four strokes. The organist begins a voluntary and the priest joins the choir in the vestry.

The church may by now have some seventy people

in it, including one or two complete families and a fair proportion of young people, ex-members of the 11 a.m. service.

The choir enters the church and the priest with his server follows as soon as the first hymn (which is taken, unannounced, from a notice-board) begins. The setting of Merbecke in response to the Ten Commandments or the Summary is used and the service follows its normal course. The sermon, preceded by notices and short Bidding Prayer, immediately follows the Nicene Creed. Then comes another hymn, the presentation of the alms and the offering of the oblations, which have been prepared during the singing of the first hymn. All stand for the Sursum Corda.· A profound silence succeeds the Prayer of Consecration, broken by the Agnus Dei. During the administration another hymn is sung softly, and afterwards all stand once more for the music of the Gloria. Finally, after the Blessing, there comes one more hymn, during which priest, server and choir pass into the vestry.

Such is an outline-picture of a Parish Communion. On the first Sunday of the month perhaps half those present will file into the hall behind the large folding doors for the parish breakfast. This has been prepared by volunteers who have had the opportunity of worshipping in the Communion at 7.30.

Here is a social fellowship in close relationship with the spiritual one of the previous hour. One does not find anything quite like this fellowship at any other social gathering. It is hoped that it may be possible in the near future to convert this monthly breakfast into a weekly one.

During the breakfast the church will again be filling

with the older boys and girls who have come for the 11 a.m. Celebration. They are not taught that they must only come and receive if fasting. The writer's position in this matter is that fasting before Communion is "an ancient and laudable custom," a means of "preparation" to "be used or not used according to every man's conscience in the sight of God" (1928 rubric). Therefore the custom is not pressed as obligatory, especially in cases where reception might otherwise be prevented.

For further details of this Young People's Communion service readers, if interested, may like to refer to *The Family of Christ's Church* (Mowbray).

What is the general effect upon parochial life of a Parish Communion from the standpoint of a new district? It might be summarised as follows:—

(1) There is now a real *centre* to all parish life and work. Do you want to come to *the* Family Service? Then come at nine. Here all important announcements are made. From those who come at 9 can be drawn the officers required to staff parish organisations in every branch of parochial life. To this service the choir comes with admirable regularity.

(2) Here also is a bond of unity between Anglo-Catholics and Evangelicals (to use the party names). The Anglo-Catholic, who is accustomed to see the Mass exalted as the chief vehicle of worship, finds the same ideal expressed in the Parish Communion. The Evangelical, who wishes to see a true "brotherhood of believers" gathered round the Lord's Table, sees such a brotherhood in the Parish Communion, for

nearly every one who comes at 9 receives then. In a new district this is a matter of very great and unusual importance, for to such parishes come men of every shade of religious conviction, ranging from the extremes of Romanism on the one hand to those of Nonconformity on the other.

It is an interesting and wonderful thing to note how both extremes are able to find unity in the " Nine o'clock." Is not this in itself a sign that this movement is of God?

(3) When those who have not worshipped for years come to the Parish Communion, one is not afraid of the result of attendance upon them. There will not be a long lesson from one of the minor prophets nor will there be (say) the 89th Psalm, things excellent in their setting (that of a thanksgiving for instructed Church people who have made their Communion earlier), but most unsuitable for the neophyte groping after the best way of adoring God. Here in the Parish Communion is worship—worship which means the adoration of an eternal Father revealed in an incarnate Son.

(4) One more effect discernible in the parish is the way in which boys and girls seem to find contentment and power of spiritual expression in the Parish Communion. We are finding that an increasing number of them, after a longer or shorter period of instruction at the 11 a.m. service, are transferring to the " Nine o'clock." They have found a way of worship which, it is believed, they could never have found in Morning or Evening Prayer.

One hesitates to give any figures. It is so easy to

exaggerate or to mislead. Nevertheless, for the encouragement of others who may contemplate the establishment of a Parish Communion, the following figures are given for what they are worth.

Taking all three celebrations together, the average number of Sunday communicants in each successive year has been as follows:—

In 1932........................... 23 per Sunday.
" 1933............................ 51 "   "
" 1934............................ 66 "   "
" 1935............................ 94 "   "
" 1936............................ 104 "   "
" 1937............................ 116 "   "

We can turn to the parable of the leaven. When the Parish Communion is made central, it does appear that God will give, in His good time and way, a visible increase, for which we may humbly thank Him, trusting that, in the end, this little leaven may leaven the whole mass of over 8000 souls.

With regard to the proportion of communicants at the Parish Communion when other Celebrations are also held, it may be of interest to record that at the Harvest Thanksgiving held in October 1937 there were 33 communicants at 7.30, 30 at 11 and 148 at 9 a.m. (On this occasion 120, including Scouts and Guides, stayed for the breakfast.)   Does not such a proportion, on an occasion when many would be present who communicate only rarely, prove the attraction of the Parish Communion, an attraction which can draw even those to whom 9 o'clock is an unfamiliar service hour?

Of course the priests in the new districts are in an

enviable position. They can bring into effect the great change which the Parish Communion means far more easily than can the incumbents of the older parishes. But when one hears of the decline in the number of many congregations and of mere handfuls present at Celebrations, one longs to be able to say, " Start with a small nucleus of faithful communicants at one great central service. Tell them that here is to be found a centre of both individual and corporate life in Christ. Ask them to come to this service if they come to no other. Ask them to bring other people. Then leave all with God! "

If one had once again the task of building up family life in a new district such as this, a precisely similar method would be used. Not Sunday School or Evening Prayer would first be announced, but a Parish Communion.

From that all else would follow. Sunday School teachers, when a school was in due course necessary. The worshippers at Evening Prayer (the thanksgiving for the blessings of Communion, the conclusion of the Church's round of worship). Churchwardens, sidesmen, the first Parochial Church Council—all these would be drawn from the original worshippers at the Parish Communion.

The foundation of the spiritual Temple of the Lord would have been laid.

What of evangelisation itself? Surely this matter of the Parish Communion is still vital. The way by which seekers may find God would seem to lie along some such lines as these. The attractive power of the life of a family whose roots are in Christ. A desire to join that family life. Attendance at some sort of enquirers' meeting. Perhaps there is coupled with this attendance at a genuine mission service (not truncated Evensong). Confirmation classes. Confirmation. The Parish Communion. To which in the end may be added the prologue or sequel of Morning or Evening Prayer.

From the standpoint of this vital matter of evangelisation, the position, as the writer sees it, is that when a soul has been brought, by whatever means, to wish to worship the Father, that soul must be brought in due course to the highest form of worship—the worship which our Lord Himself ordained when He said, " Do this in remembrance of Me."

Such worship is in itself an evangelising power which may, under God, be trusted to complete a process of conversion already begun.

E

5

FROM OTHER PROVINCES

(A) AUSTRALIA

By P. A. Micklem

As Rector of St. James', Sydney, for twenty years from 1917 till 1937, I am glad to have been asked to write a short account of the place which this church occupies in the great city of Sydney, and indeed in Australia as a whole. Built nearly 120 years ago by a convict architect, and with convict labour, it stands with its lofty steeple in the very centre of the mother city of Australia, in that part of the city, too, within which are concentrated its business life and the great spheres of government and politics, of medicine and law. Daily there flock into this city area from the suburbs of Sydney, near and far, the public servants of New South Wales, the barristers and solicitors of the State, its specialists in medicine and surgery, its bankers and men of commerce, together with the hundreds of men and women employed in the banks and business offices. On the other hand, it is an area which contains a relatively small resident population—caretakers, members of hotel staffs, etc., the nature of whose work necessitates their living on the premises where their work is done.

Thus St. James' is a typical city church, with, however, unique opportunities of spiritual witness to the multitudes which daily pass its doors, and whose daily work is done in the immediate neighbourhood. Hence the importance of the week-day activities of the church. Day by day, and throughout the day, its doors are open, and its quiet interior is constantly used for rest and prayer. Day by day the Holy Eucharist is celebrated and the morning and evening offices are said; and throughout the year short services are regularly held at mid-day during the business lunch hour, at which addresses and instructions are given.

But St. James' is far more than a city church in the sense above described, for, in addition to its week-day activities, it has a large permanent congregation, the members of which are drawn to it from all parts of Sydney, and regard it as their parish and spiritual home. Indeed, it has sometimes been called the Parish Church of Australia; for to it and to its services regularly come visitors from the other states, and from the more distant parts of New South Wales, expecting and finding there the type of worship which they desire. It is, however, folk living in the nearer and more remote suburbs of Sydney who form the permanent nucleus of its worshippers, and who come specially within the scope of its pastoral activities. For them the attraction of the old church lies, apart from the life of keen fellowship of which it is the centre, in the Catholic teaching which is there given, and the standard of sober and dignified Catholic worship which is there maintained. The central service of the week is the solemn Eucharist as offered on Sundays at 11 a.m., when the liturgy is presented with those accompaniments of ceremonial which research in recent years has shown to be traditional in the English Church.

It is, however, of the 9 o'clock Eucharist at St. James' that I desire to speak in conclusion. For it is this service, more than any other, which is characteristic of the church, and which also perhaps in a special degree exemplifies the Parish Communion, the extension of which it is the object of this book to advocate. Nearly forty years ago, during the Rectorship of the late Rev. W. I. Carr-Smith, it was seen that if the Eucharist was to be given a central place in the affections and devotions of the people of the parish, it must be offered at an hour not too early for the convenience of those living in the suburbs, and at the same time not too late for them to make their communion fasting. Hence the institution of the Parish Eucharist at 9 o'clock, a service sung congregationally to a simple setting, and at which an average of 130 to 140 worshippers make their communion. A short address, of not more than seven minutes, is given from the chancel steps, and the whole service is concluded at 10 o'clock, or a few minutes later. Nor is it too much to say that countless visitors from other parts of the world who have found their way to this service have been deeply struck with the ordered beauty and reverent devotion which characterise it. The service is followed immediately by a Communion breakfast arranged for in the large crypt, which, with its vaulted chambers, occupies the whole area of the church below its floor level. This simple meal, for which a small charge is made, provides a most welcome opportunity for social fellowship between communicants living at considerable distances from each other and for meeting the clergy;

and the combination of Parish Eucharist and breakfast is so deeply rooted in the life of St. James' and in the affections of its people, that it is safe to say that, whatever changes may occur in other directions, this will remain.

It should perhaps be added that coincidently with the 9 o'clock Eucharist in the main church is also celebrated a Eucharist for children in the beautiful little children's chapel, with its frescoed walls and ceiling, in the crypt of the church. Here the smaller children are brought by their parents in order that they may learn how to worship, by worshipping at their own simply sung Eucharist, the Eucharist being followed by a short period of instruction, after which they rejoin their parents, who in many cases have been present at the Eucharist celebrated at the High Altar in the main church.

(B) INDIA

By C. H. HEMMING

THE parish priest in Simla was, years ago, confronted with a community sharply divided into sections with very little intercommunication. The idea of a Christian brotherhood, a Christian family embracing all the faithful was, in these circumstances, almost non-existent. Not only was there the exclusiveness as between the European, Anglo-Indian and Indian, but different sections of the European community—the Government official and the non-official, the "covenanted" and the "uncovenanted" person—were poles apart. "Bridge the gulf" societies and clubs made attempts to overcome this unpleasant state of things, but it seemed to us that the Church was really the one Society to accomplish it. Our effort was first of all to make the Christian fellowship a reality, and it seemed to us the one way to accomplish that was by definite teaching of the place the Blessed Sacrament, the Sacrament of Fellowship, should occupy in the normal Christian life.

The tradition at Christ Church, Simla, was of a Celebration of Holy Communion every Saint's Day and on one week-day besides; and on Sunday always a Celebration at 8 a.m., Mattins at 11 a.m., with an occasional late Celebration and a Celebration once a month at 7. The 8 o'clock Celebration was very well attended when I was in charge at Simla, and the numbers of communicants considerable. But the good souls present were, so it seemed to us, a gathering making individual acts of worship, with little, if any, realisation of their corporate existence. They were not a family at worship. What we set out to try to do first of all was to recover or create the idea of " the Church that was in Simla " at worship the first day of the week at Holy Communion.

We started to try to break down this exclusiveness by forming a simple " Fellowship." Members were to make a monthly Corporate Communion with special intention, and afterwards breakfast together—share in a kind of agape—and so get to know one another. We did not alter the time of the Holy Communion service, which seemed to suit the greater number of our people.

There was, at first, a certain amount of opposition. It was held by some that the circumstances of Simla society, with its strong official element, were not suitable for an experiment of this sort.

However, from the outset the idea appealed to many, and numbers steadily grew, and I believe parishioners did begin to get a real sense of Christian fellowship.

It was a happy sight to see the Bishop of the diocese, heads of departments of Army headquarters, school teachers, senior officials in the Indian Civil Service, clerks in Government offices, both Anglo-Indians and Europeans, Indians, shopkeepers and others trooping from their communion to the school hard by the church where the Fellowship breakfast was served.

We had no financial difficulties. There was a box at the door for gifts towards expenses, and I had previously persuaded my Church Committee that the realisation of what was meant by the fellowship in Christ Jesus was one of the most important bits of our work as a congregation, and that money spent upon it was better spent than, for instance, on new kneelers or even new hymn-books.

I left Simla when we had got as far as this. I don't know whether or not the Fellowship still exists.

(c) SCOTLAND

By R. M. GRIER

ONE of the earliest pioneers in introducing the " Agape " after the congregational Mass on Sunday was Provost Smythe of St. Ninian's, Perth. The Episcopal Church in Scotland once was in defined parishes. Disendowed by William III for political reasons, the

Church has had in the succeeding centuries to build new churches and new cathedrals. In Perth there are two, the Cathedral and the Church of St. John. The congregations number in all about 1600 or 1700, where the individual members are scattered over a city of 30,000 and are also to be found in the outlying country. They also differ, as is natural, in status and in wealth. In the poorer part of Perth the Cathedral has a flourishing mission room, which is most efficiently run by the Church Army. But it is not consecrated, and all who go there for mission services come for their communions to the Cathedral.

Provost Smythe ever taught at Kettering that the Blessed Sacrament was the centre of Catholic life. On coming to Perth he found that this was already known through the teaching of the saintly Bishop Wilkinson and his helpers. The new Provost set himself to make it easy and possible for all his varied and widely scattered congregation to attend the Lord's Service on the Lord's Day. So, in addition to the usual daily and Sunday said Masses, he introduced a 9 o'clock sung Eucharist each Sunday. This enabled people to come in from outside Perth by bus or motor, and also allowed those whose weekly work often ended late on Saturday night to have a well-earned rest.

To the development of this service as the congregation's act of worship he gave much of his great ability for organisation. In every way he encouraged his people to come to it, and unremitting labour was not in vain. Although many must originally have attended through their personal love for the man and priest, he laid such sound foundations that the service is still the best attended of all on Sunday. The music is always simple, and Merbecke is invariably sung, together with well-known and suitable English Hymnal hymns. A voluntary ladies' choir, assisted by members of the Cathedral choir, and with the organist, leads the singing. The ritual is dignified and un-ostentatious. The celebrant is attended by two servers and a ceremonarius. A brief address, generally on the Gospel, is given from the chancel step. The number of communicants on an ordinary Sunday varies from seventy-five to 120. The whole is essentially a congregational service of worship and communion.

At the same time, it was essential to provide breakfast for the communicants who are taught to observe the discipline of the Church in fasting before Mass. Both those who had come from a distance and also families who had shut up their homes had to be thought of. So the verger began by supplying breakfast in the Chapter House to about eight people. Now the numbers may be anything from thirty to over 100. Old and young, rich and poor, Provost and choir-boy, and sometimes Bishops, all sit down to break-fast—and a very good breakfast it is. There is a choice of scrambled eggs, fish or sausages, bread, butter, marmalade, jam and tea. The cost is sixpence a head. It is provided by a member of the Cathedral. But no one knows how it is done—we are content to realise that it is done. Such a meal, simple and democratic, has all the elements of a true agape. This is even more apparent on the greater festivals and on those Sundays when there is a Corporate Communion of Servers, Scottish Mothers' Union and such like. After grace has been said by the Provost, there is a buzz of conversation from all, who do feel they are bound together in a real fellowship.

This short description shows what can be done, and also how from small beginnings a great and sound work can grow. There is no doubt that such a combined service and refreshment goes far to enhance both the spiritual and social life of the congregation. For the true Catholic both are inextricably bound together. The parochial or congregational difficulty has been to bring this about. There are those who fear that such an hour would discourage abstinence; I think there is far more fear lest a service at an unsuitable hour should discourage attendance altogether. Others may feel that such a service demands too much from a single-handed priest. But if such a service can draw so many to a cathedral in addition to its other four or five services on Sunday, it is well worth attempting anywhere.

(D) A SOUTH AFRICAN MISSION

By Philip Stroud, S.S.M.

The Church's worship is ultimately a unity, as the Church herself is one, but the Church and her worship must be adapted to the varying requirements of her environment, and to the customs and ways of thought of her members. Obvious as this statement may appear, its implications are not always easy to work out or to accept. It is not easy, perhaps one may say it ought not to be easy, to feel at home in the liturgy as celebrated in an Indian, an African or a Chinese

Church, even though the framework of the service is that of the Book of Common Prayer. It is easy to see irreverence where there is none, or to see formalism simply because the forms are not our own. Missionaries, though in many ways favourably placed, are not always able to distinguish between what is Catholic and essential, and what is merely English and insular. A visitor to an Indian mission station " remarked rapturously, without noticing the left-handedness of the praise, ' How delightfully English,' whereas the best commendation he could give would be not to feel at home there. For the first thing you see of a man is his clothing; only later do you penetrate to his soul. Let the visitor through a totally ' different-from-home ' exterior finally penetrate to the true Christian soul and find himself at one there. That would be a satisfying conclusion, an assurance that things were on the right lines." [1]

So when attempting to describe what in England has come to be called the Parish Communion, *i.e.* the Communion as the great service of the Sunday, South African conditions must first be taken into account. The background of native life, and of native Church life in particular, is different; the outward form, at least the service and the attitude of the people towards it, are different. First among the differences is the fact that no native Church Christian can conceive of any other as the chief service and the normal service of the Church, even though his opportunities of attending it are usually few.

Obviously the time of the service depends entirely on local conditions. It can be the same service with

[1] *O.M.C. Quarterly Paper*, July 1936.

the same underlying ideals of worship in India at 6,
in England at 9.30, in South Africa at 10.30 or 11.30.[1]

There are in the Orange Free State two main
groups among the native people: those of small
towns (dorps) and those of the farms. The dorp
natives live in locations distinct from, but not usually
far removed from, the European towns. They include
a few, teachers and others, with sufficient education
to read and write. The majority are servants in
European homes, or are labourers of various sorts.
The hours of work vary in different occupations and
in different homes, but it is usually possible for them
to be at Mass on their one (or possibly two) Sundays
a month at or about 10.30.

The farm natives live in small groups of four or
five huts on European farms, sometimes at considerable distances, ten or twenty miles, from the church.
They, too, can usually manage to be at Mass on their
one Sunday at about 10.30. The time, especially in
winter, is not strictly adhered to. At farm centres,
Mass may be anything from one to one and a half
hours late. It begins when the people have arrived.
It is rather trying to the European to see, miles away
over the veld, an ox waggon with a considerable
proportion of the congregation, and to know that he
can do nothing till it arrives. The rest of the congregation do not worry.

There are cases in the towns, due to the conditions
of work and the common lack of consideration for
natives, where people cannot come at 10 o'clock.

[1] Even though the usual hour of service in our missions is so
late, the fast before Communion is observed. We have plenty of
evidence of this; and it is not uncommon at other times for the
native to go without food till quite late in the day.

For these people a Mass at 4 a.m. is arranged from time to time, and many of the congregation come to it. At great festivals in Bloemfontein, practically everyone comes to the 4 o'clock High Mass, and most of them make their communion then.

In some ways Bloemfontein is very similar to a large English town parish. 28,000 natives live in the location. But there are some important differences. St. Patrick's Church has a number of catechists, readers and subdeacons, each responsible for a district in the location. Many of the people, too, come from the country or from small dorps where conditions are very different from the English parish, and much of their attitude to the Church is brought with them.

Except in Bloemfontein, the town natives, though not so poor as those on the farms, are very poor. Yet on the whole they pay their Church dues very well. These are one shilling a month for men and sixpence a month for women.

The farm natives are very often paid largely in kind. It is estimated that ten shillings to fifteen shillings a month is the commonest money wage, representing roughly 30 per cent. of the full wage, the remainder being made up of rations and a certain amount of land. Out of this the Government takes poll-tax. Church dues are on the whole well paid; to the never-ending amazement of the missionaries. It is a sign, however, of their love for their Church, and perhaps of the value they set on the social side of Church life. It is frequently said by Europeans that " the natives love their Church Sunday. It's their great social occasion." The comment is not unkindly meant, and is certainly a true one. It is a

matter for rejoicing that the Church is the centre of
what little social life there is, for the farm natives'
interests are very narrow; very few can read. Because
of the lack of stimulus, they are not merely ignorant,
but also frequently dull and slow of understanding.
From month to month they see very few people outside their own family circle and that of their " baas."
Their movements are restricted by pass laws; under a
harsh and unsympathetic farmer, it may be very
difficult for them to get about at all.

On some farms there are farm schools, usually with
not very well qualified teachers, but even then, as
small boys are often used for herding cattle, it frequently
happens that they get to school, if at all, at too late
an age. Natives have no free education.

Such are the people who come month by month
to take their part in the worship of the Church of
God.

There are certain elements in Church life itself very
different from the Church life of an English parish.
One of the most important is the attitude of the people
to the Bishop. " Our Bishop " may be a long way
away, but he is to the people very truly their Father
in God. He is a great person, but he is a great person whom they know. They are respectful to their
priest, though no doubt aberrations in his Sesuto, or
whatever is the language of the district, may cause
amusement; but they know that the real father of
the family is the Bishop. It is no small thing that in
this country of colour bar and race prejudice Europeans, Basuto, Bechuana and Ama Xosa have the
one Father in God.

The priest's visits are infrequent—once a month in

the larger centres, elsewhere bi-monthly or when opportunity offers. The disadvantages—and the wrongness—of this are apparent, but there are great compensating advantages. Where the priest is permanently resident, the people are inclined to leave matters to him, and he is perhaps too inclined to let it be so. Where people have never been accustomed to have the priest permanently, there is much more of a sense of the Church. The catechist and the older members of the congregation take their part in the Church's life and work. They report to the priest any grievous sin that has become known, and advise him how to deal with it. They advise, too, on matters connected with Church dues. They search out the sick and pray with them. The women, with no urging from the priest, undertake the cleaning of the church, usually prefacing their work with some devotions. The catechist and others instruct the young and the hearers and catechumens. Besides the last two-mentioned grades, there is another not known to England—that of penitents. All alike are looking forward to the time when they will be admitted or restored to Communion. There are usually classes for them on Sundays. On the Mass Sunday, they usually follow the Mass. The priest cannot take them all, but he questions and examines them as to fitness for signing, baptism or restoration as the case may be.

One very important element in Church life calls for comment. There is still a barrier between people of different tribes, such as Barolong and Basuto, and in a congregation where both are strongly represented there may be frequent friction. But when a person moves from one district to another, even if only for a

visit, he takes from his priest or catechist a Church
letter, setting forth his grade of membership, and,
when he is to reside permanently in the new district,
the amount he has paid in Church dues. When he
arrives at the new place, he presents the letter at the
earliest opportunity to the priest. Very often, some of
the congregation, even if they are of a different tribe,
will let the priest know that there is a visitor of the
Church staying at So-and-so's house. He is accepted
immediately as a brother.

The family feeling of the native Church is a difficult
thing to convey in words, but it is very strong. It is
as a family, a brotherhood, that the Church comes
together month by month for the great service, some
from the nearby location, some from a distance, some
on horseback, some in Cape carts, some on foot, some
in European dress, some well-dressed, some in rags,
and others in colourful blankets, old men and young,
women and girls. They sit outside the church, in the
shade in summer, in the sun in winter, talking to their
friends and relatives whom perhaps they have not
seen since last month. When they meet the priest,
there is much handshaking and many greetings. Inside the church, if it is a large Mission, there are a few
men and boys preparing the altar, the incense and
themselves. The congregation comes in by ones and
twos, and there is silence in the church save for the
occasional cry of a child on its mother's back. The
women sit on one side, the men on the other. There
may be baptisms or even a wedding, beforehand, or
perhaps the restoration of penitents. Whatever it is,
it is the business of the whole congregation. The
responses of the Baptism office are said by all who know

them, godparents or not, and so even with the Church-
ing of Women.

The Mass follows. The Bantu have a natural
aptitude for harmony; so, though the hymn book has
plainsong settings for Creed and Gloria, etc., all is
sung in improvised harmony, which is often reminiscent
of Russian Orthodox services. Hymns are sung at the
usual places in the service, and are begun by the
catechist and taken up by the congregation. There is
no choir and no instrumental accompaniment. As
many of the congregation cannot read or do not
possess hymn-books, some of the hymns are almost
invariables and are sung by heart.

If there is a subdeacon present, he may read the
Epistle. The sermon usually follows the Gospel, and
is almost invariably a simple exposition of the Collect,
Epistle or Gospel. As a rule it is given in English and
interpreted, sometimes into two other languages; it
must be simple, with one plain point well hammered
home. In large towns, something different is required,
but in the Orange Free State most of the churches are
in small dorps or farm centres.

At the Offertory prayers will be asked for sick persons,
for rain (a matter of great importance) or some other
object easily visualised. The collection is not quite so
important as in England, owing to the system of
Church dues. It often affords, however, an example
of the naturalness of Church life. There is rarely a
bag or a " decent bason," so the collection will be
made on a catechist's open hymn-book or in a cup.
Once I have seen it taken in a hat. Other examples
of naturalness spring to mind. A mother will uncon-
cernedly feed her baby if it cries during Mass. At

F

Communion she may either bring the baby with her on her back, or hand it to someone near her to hold till she returns to her place.

The Confession is led by a subdeacon or a catechist, the people saying each phrase after him. Here, where he knows his way, the full Sesuto inflexions are made. To hear Subdeacon Sefatsa lead the confession is a liberal education.

Then the Preface, for which the people stand. The Creed, earlier in the service, being somewhat elaborate, may have been rather raggedly sung; but the Sanctus is well known. Now all kneel again, well aware that the central act is coming. In the South African rite, the Consecration, Oblation and Lord's Prayer follow immediately. If he knows nothing else, the native knows how to sing the Lord's Prayer.

At the Communion, the men receive first. In some places, there is a subdeacon to whom the right of administering the Chalice has been granted—a great honour, and highly esteemed. Meanwhile the Agnus and some Communion hymns are sung. After the first row, a catechist or some chief man marshals the communicants quietly and unobtrusively, that all may be orderly.

So the service draws to an end. There is no unseemly rush out. Very often the priest leads a few short prayers of thanksgiving. After that, there are many things to be done. There may be sick communions to be taken to people in the location, receiving of Church monies, reports of falls into open sin, and so on; and all this takes time, interrupted as it is by greetings from various people not seen before Mass. All explanations of things take time: the point is not often approached directly. Meanwhile the catechists are conducting classes. The priest keeps half an eye on them, questions some and perhaps arranges to baptize or admit some to the catechumenate next month.

Outside the church, horses are being inspanned, men and women in their respective circles are talking, babies are being fed, some are having their meals before going away to their farm; and when at last the priest comes out there is much getting up from the ground, a dusting of hands on trouser leg or blankets and on voluminous skirts and then a chorus of " Dumela Ntate," and the Mass is over for a month.

6

HOW A COVENTRY CHURCH MADE THE VENTURE

BY H. C. JAMES

My church—mine of course in a very limited sense—stands principally for something which in modern times is still somewhat unusual—namely, the endeavour to centralise the whole parish life in a corporate, weekly, act of Communion, known as the Parish Eucharist.

I should indeed fail in the purpose of this article if it were to be supposed that by the Parish Eucharist is meant anything other than the Holy Communion of the English Prayer Book, and of the whole Catholic Church. That great heritage is common to us all, and is our centre of unity. Where we do differ, one parish from another, is in the use which we make of it. Equally it is far from my intention to claim that the *details* of a plan such as ours are possible or advisable for parishes in general. My real aim is to set forth some of the considerations which lie behind our particular plan, and which make it the outward expression of a great spiritual ideal.

The fundamental assumption is that the Holy Catholic Church is one vast family existing for one supreme purpose—namely, the worship and service of Almighty God. Worship may be described as the right and necessary attitude of a human being in the presence of his Maker. Acts of worship are needed to express that attitude and to foster it, and the chief act of Christian worship is the Eucharist or " breaking of bread," which from the earliest days has been the characteristic feature of Christian gatherings.

These gatherings were family gatherings of all the members of Christ in the town or village. None would absent himself save for the gravest reason, and the worship which was offered was corporate worship. All would join in the prayers and praises and in the central act of communion. Their worship was not so much a " service " as an action, in which each one had a part to play, and from them we learn what the Eucharist really is—namely, a whole society doing something before God. That this primitive Christian worship had its social side, in which the members enjoyed a common fellowship, is clear both from the New Testament and from the early history of the Church.

How different in these all-important respects is the general Eucharistic worship of to-day! Too often the impression given by the early Celebration on Sunday is of a gathering of separate individuals almost cherishing their isolation, rather than of a corporate body sharing in a joyful family occasion.

The sung Eucharist, on the other hand, held, as it often is, in the middle of the morning, almost of necessity lacks the vital act of Communion, the eating and drinking together which are of the essence of the Sacrament, and which express and deepen the unity of family life; and what great opportunities are missed by the immediate dispersal of the congregation after the service is over!

The natural sequel to family worship is family intercourse, by means of which friendships are made and cemented in the atmosphere of worship already created by the Eucharist. Instead, whilst some of the members may linger for a hand-shake or a few words, the majority go their ways in ones and twos as they came. It is not an exaggeration to say that communicants at the same altar over a period of years sometimes do not know one another even by name.

A plan such as ours overcomes most of these drawbacks, and has, in addition, many practical advantages. But before coming down to a detailed description of it, I would first say something about the parish itself, which is almost entirely industrial, and which has a population of 10,000.

Founded in 1848, it first came under the direct influence of the Catholic Revival in the year 1909. At that time a daily Celebration was started, and in 1914 the principal service on Sunday mornings at 11 was changed from Mattins to the sung Eucharist. This was the arrangement which I found in 1921, and with which we persevered until 1927. The congregation was never a large one, even though it included numbers of children, but this was not so disturbing as the conviction, which grew as the years went by, that there must be something lacking in a plan for Sunday morning which invited the faithful to the Lord's Table twice and sometimes three times, and yet, so far as Communion was concerned, sent more than half of them empty away.

I will not dwell upon the imperfections of what is now to us here the old régime. They may be summed up by saying that the Blessed Sacrament, given by our Lord for one purpose above all others, was used principally for something less than, and secondary to, that purpose.

Could anything be done about it? That was the question constantly in my mind, and at last the answer came from St. Mary's, Portsea, through its then vicar, the Rev. J. F. L. Southam, who in a lecture to clergy at which I was privileged to be present, described the Parish Eucharist and breakfast as he then had it in his own parish. That was some twelve or thirteen years ago. I went back to my people and told them the good news, preaching and talking about it as often as I could during the next two years, at the end of which time I framed a questionnaire asking them if they were in favour of such a change, and whether it might be effected in the near future. Of 200 replies sent in 115 were in favour, and 85 against. This was not the unanimity that could have been desired, but an examination of the " Noes " revealed that the great majority were people who communicated infrequently, and who made no use of the church on Sunday morning after the early Celebrations. In these circumstances I felt justified in proceeding, and after a period of intensive teaching and preparation, on Whitsun Day, 1927, we changed our Sunday morning plan by moving the 11 o'clock sung Eucharist back to 9.15 and following it with breakfast in the Parish Room. We did lose, to my regret, a few regular members of the 11 o'clock congregation, not because (saving in one or two cases) they disapproved of the change, but for practical reasons, which made their attendance at 9.15 impossible.

So great a venture was bound to involve some degree of loss. On the other hand, quite a number of those who voted against the change soon became, and are still among, its most devoted adherents.

The Service

I will now describe the service in some detail. We deliberately gave up the more elaborate musical settings and chose Martin Shaw's Modal Mass (Curwen, 6d.), which we have used ever since. The choir made no difficulty about this, and the attendance at 9.15 both of men and boys has always been good. There are five hymns (six if there is a procession), and the congregation join in the music from beginning to end. Only the senior children (eleven years and upwards) come to the Parish Eucharist, the idea being that the infants and juniors will be better provided for later in the morning, until such time as they are ready to come into the family worship without undue strain to themselves and without disturbing the quiet and concentration of others. The service lasts an hour and a quarter, so far as it is possible no more and no less. The chief variant is the length of the address. If there is a procession and a large number of communicants, it may be as short as five minutes; on ferial Sundays there is usually time for a quarter of an hour. Immediately after the Prayer of Consecration all sing, softly, the two verses of " Wherefore, O Father " (E.H. 335). This, with the

Amen which follows, gives the people an added sense of co-operation with the celebrant in the act of consecration, and brings the prayer itself to a more natural conclusion. After a period of silence is sung the Agnus Dei, and then the Communion begins, first of the servers and choir, then of the people. In order to avoid the long lines of waiting communicants so familiar at said Celebrations on great feasts, a churchwarden regulates their approach to the altar in the simplest possible manner by standing in the centre aisle facing the altar, and moving back a few rows at a time. Only those in front of him leave their places, the rest waiting until he stands behind the pew in which they are kneeling. At the conclusion of the service, the celebrant, having taken off the chasuble, returns to the chancel step, where he leads a brief thanksgiving out of the communion manuals with which all are provided.

The Breakfast

I said that the Vicar of Portsea solved our problem of non-communicating attendance, but he did more than that. I had never heard of the Parish Eucharist breakfast, and it is to this that I turn now at some length because of its tremendous value and importance. When I first saw and admired it at St. Mary's, Portsea, I was quite sure that its introduction would be impossible here, and I tried hard to get Mr. Southam to agree. I cannot be too thankful that he refused to do so, but it was with a somewhat faint heart that I returned home prepared if need be to pick a crust with two or three faithful people who would offer themselves for the experiment. Imagine my joy when on the first Sunday morning we sat down to our repast seventy strong, and when as the weeks and months sped by it became evident that the breakfast had come to stay. Parochial teas and the like are good, but this is better. To breakfast in the company of those with whom only just before you had partaken of the Bread of Life is to realise vividly and afresh the benign Fatherhood of God and the happy family life in which, through our Lord Jesus Christ, we share as His children. When this has been said, it seems almost trivial to come down to practical and social advantages, but they are so implicit and of such great import that I beg leave to describe them. In the first place, the breakfast is a witness and an aid to fasting communion. I will only say here, with regard to this important matter, that its desirability is emphatically taught, and that the breakfast to my certain knowledge greatly facilitates its practice. Secondly, I estimate that but for the breakfast quite 25 per cent. of those who came to the Parish Eucharist would be unable to do so. There simply would be no breakfast for them when they returned home late in the morning, without serious inconvenience to themselves and to others. Thirdly, it brings together people who otherwise would know little or nothing of each other. Nearly everyone comes to it, and strangers are given a cordial invitation at the end of the Eucharist by the clergy and churchwardens. Lastly, the breakfast greatly assists the working of the parish machine. Additional notices are given out, work is arranged, and plans are discussed, whilst afterwards committees are able to meet, and clergy and people have unique access to each other for the hundred and one purposes of parish life.

It would be difficult to imagine any parochial organisation which runs more smoothly and easily. Our experience has been that a committee of one is all that is required. This committee (with us it has always been a lady) distributes the necessary work among some twenty-four to thirty helpers who are divided into teams, each being on duty once in seven or eight weeks. She herself does the catering, keeps the accounts, and has the custody of the crockery, table-cloths, bread-cutter, etc., belonging to the breakfast. The menu consists of tea and coffee, jam and marmalade, potted meat and cut bread and butter. A collecting box is passed round during the meal, and a nominal charge of threepence is made. It is true that some people give in excess of this amount, but the striking fact remains that the breakfast not only pays for itself, but also buys its own crockery, knives and table-cloths. On Sunday morning those on duty make their Communion at 8 o'clock, but on special occasions they have found it possible both to prepare the breakfast and also to be present at the Eucharist. How this is done is one of the mysteries which are beyond the wit of a mere man. Grace is said corporately before breakfast, but not after, the people dispersing at will when they have finished. Smoking is permitted at the end of the meal. Clearing away and washing up are usually finished by 11.30.

After breakfast the Social Club is thrown open to all who have been present in church, and in winter especially a number of people avail themselves of it.

I have written at some length about the breakfast,

because there are to my knowledge a number of parishes which have or are contemplating the Eucharist without it. To such I would earnestly say: Give it a trial, wholeheartedly, enthusiastically, optimistically; if you fail, no damage surely will be done; if you succeed, as I believe you will, the gain to the Eucharist and to the general life of the parish will be incalculable. Here it has been so easy and so happy and useful that were I to move, I would try for it in almost any circumstances, even though the nearest suitable room were at a distance from the church; and even though the numbers were small, I should be confident that it would enable at least a few more to come to the Eucharist, and would foster that family spirit in Church life which is so much to be desired.

Results

I come now to results, of which I write with some diffidence, but without which an essay such as this would be incomplete. The Parish Eucharist is no quick or easy means to success. Nevertheless, looking back over ten years, I see that from the very beginning it brought us two blessings which could scarcely have come in any other way. The first was the doubling of the number of the Sunday communicants— the doubling, that is, of those who, being possessed by Christ in His Sacrament, bear Him forth to their fellows in the world. The second was the unique fellowship of the breakfast. These, coming to us as they did on Whitsun Day, 1927, were a veritable Pentecostal gift. With this new material, and by means of this " flying start," we have been enabled,

slowly but surely, to enrich and to extend the whole
of our parish life, and the joy with which each succeeding anniversary has been celebrated is eloquent
of the grace belonging to this modern, yet primitive
Christian ideal.

Although ideally the Parish Eucharist is the for-
gathering of all the communicant members, in practice we have found it necessary to continue the said
Celebration at 8 o'clock. Comparatively few come
to this, but it enables the breakfast helpers to make
their communion on their Sunday of duty, and also
meets the needs of some others who are unable to
come at 9.15. The ages of those who come to the
Parish Eucharist range fairly evenly between eleven
and the fifties, with perhaps a preponderance on the
side of youth, together with some representatives of
the sixties and seventies. A record has not been kept
of the numbers at breakfast, but the average is probably between sixty and seventy.

The important question will be asked, How does
this Sunday morning arrangement affect the Sunday
School and the children? The answer is not easy to
give because of the great changes which have come
over Sunday School life and work in recent years.
The number of children, especially in towns, has
fallen off, and there are fewer " twicers " (to say
nothing of " thricers ") than there used to be, which
means that the difficulty of their training, both in
worship and knowledge of the faith, is considerably
increased.

Nevertheless, I claim that our new plan is pro-
ducing proportionately better results than the old.
Formerly, all the children came to the sung Eucharist

at 11, and very long and difficult they found it. Moreover, it was a training in non-communicating attendance which could only lead to perplexity in years to
come. What now happens is that the infants and
juniors have a service in church from 11.30 to 12.15.
The seniors, to whom reference has already been
made, obviously appreciate the privilege of coming to
the Parish Eucharist, at which they take their places
not grouped together, but among the general congregation. The afternoon arrangements are unchanged,
the seniors being in church, and the juniors and
infants in Sunday School.

I come now to what are generally known as the
" young people," *i.e.* those between the ages of fourteen and twenty. We find that, having regard to
the drop in numbers, a larger proportion remain
faithful to the Parish Eucharist than did to the sung
Eucharist at 11. It is a bigger thing, after the " props "
of the Sunday School have been removed, to give up
the weekly Communion, than it was to stop coming
to the sung Eucharist. Then there is the additional
attraction of the extra hour in bed if desired, and of
the convenience and fellowship of the breakfast.
Everything seems to combine to retain the adolescent,
and at the same time to set before him the highest
ideal of the life and worship of the Church. This is
not to claim that the leakage common to this period
has been stopped, but it has undoubtedly been
stemmed. I can truly say that I never before had so
many young people of outstanding quality and usefulness as at the present time, and I regard them,
with much thankfulness, as the first-fruits of the
Parish Eucharist and breakfast.

To the same cause, too, I attribute the fact that we were able in 1929 to give up the ordinary collections in church, and to concentrate on the method of the Free-Will Offering, which rose in an incredibly short time, and in spite of much poverty and unemployment, from £112 to £360 per annum. Yet another result has been a marked increase in prayer, work, and offerings for Overseas Missions.

The Parish Eucharist makes Sunday morning easier for the parish priest, if only by reason of the fact that his fast terminates at 10.30 instead of at 12 o'clock or even later. Mattins, too, is said privately, and quite half the morning is thus available for work with the children and for interviews.

One other result is worthy of mention—namely, the interest taken by other parishes. In one case representatives of a congregation thirty miles away came over twice in order to see the Parish Eucharist and breakfast, and it was my great privilege not long ago to be present at the first anniversary of its introduction in their own church. Hereabouts four churches have started the Parish Eucharist in the last few years, two of them with breakfast as well, whilst I know of several others over a wide area who are giving the matter their serious consideration.

The Future

What of the future? It is full of hope and of promise. As the years go by we hope that more and more of our members will join in this corporate weekly act of communion, until it can be truly said that the only absentees from this great family gathering of the members are those who are absolutely prevented from coming by reasons not under their control, and who long for the time when those reasons will be removed. It will need years of patient teaching on the part of the clergy, and of faithful witness by the laity, before so desirable a state of things can come about, but the ideal is there in all its beauty and power, a beginning has been made, and a large number of the communicants are definitely working by prayer and influence for its realisation. Just in proportion as we succeed will be granted to us that other blessing for which we greatly long—namely, that there shall be nothing in the parish life and work which does not owe its origin, its existence, and its inspiration to the worship and fellowship of the Eucharist. Such a community could not be narrowly parochial. Christ Himself dwelling within it would constrain the members to evangelise those with whom they come in contact in everyday life, and to co-operate in the spread of the Gospel in the city and diocese and overseas. It would find and operate the ideal solutions of the problems of Church maintenance, for the secret of that spiritual thing called Christian finance is to be found as nowhere else in the full, perfect, and complete offering of Christ on which the Eucharist is founded.

That which ten years ago was regarded as an innovation has now begun to be a tradition. None of our children under the age of fifteen can remember any other plan for Sunday morning, whilst the number of older people, to whom any change is almost always a cause of pain and grief, grows slowly but inevitably smaller. The writer believes that his successors will continue the present plan without essential alteration, partly because it is neither High Church nor Low, but Catholic, in the best sense of that much-misused word; partly because to a large number of his people it has come to mean so much; mostly because it is centred in Christ Himself, in simple obedience to the command which He gave the night on which He was betrayed.

7

A GREAT MOTHER CHURCH

By H. C. Robins

True worship and true fellowship are two essential elements in the Christian life. They give satisfaction to our true nature as children of God and members of Christ. Both are to be found in the Parish Communion followed by the parish breakfast, which links worship with fellowship after the manner of the early Church. That has certainly been our experience at Portsea, where the Parish Communion has been in existence for fifteen years, and where it was soon followed by a simple meal of fellowship. The two together are now one of the greatest inspirations of the parochial life. We owe their inception to Canon Southam, a former vicar, and they have been continued by his successor, Canon Lunt, now Bishop of Ripon, and by myself. Both are a permanent and valued part of our common life.

First let me set down a few relevant facts. Portsea is a very large parish, with a mainly working-class population. It is manned by a vicar and nine or ten assistant curates, which enables us to do things impossible for a parish with a less adequate staff. We have a very noble parish church, built under Canon

Jacob (later Bishop of Newcastle, and afterwards of St. Albans), and five daughter churches serving thickly populated districts. Our churchmanship is in the main central, but we have varieties in the way we express it in worship. Having, as I have said, a large and varied staff, we are able to make experiments in our forms of worship—as, for example, Children's Eucharists. But we all of us agree as to the value of the two People's Communions. These are held every Sunday, one at the parish church and one at a daughter church, St. Wilfrid's. Their effectiveness is proved by the request made by two other of our daughter churches to follow the example of the parish church and St. Wilfrid's, by having a People's Communion once or twice a month, and thus testing its further success in the parish. It would not, I think, be either desirable, or true to our history, to have a Parish Communion for the whole parish, except, as we do, on certain special occasions.

The hour of our Parish Communion, both at the parish church and at St. Wilfrid's, is 9.30 a.m., which seems the best hour to satisfy our particular needs. We do not force it on those who prefer other hours, but provide in addition at each of the two churches an 8 a.m. Celebration every Sunday for those who value a quieter service. The parish church also has sung Mattins and sermon every Sunday at 11.15, and a plain Celebration at 12.15 once a month. To complete the description of our Eucharistic atmosphere, the parish church has a daily Celebration during the week, and St. Wilfrid's three Celebrations and the other churches two during each week, in addition to those on Sunday.

That is the sort of parish we are—with a long tradition of worship, neither very High nor very Low—just, as was said most unfairly of the Scots, " the happy mean "! I am most thankful to add that we are a parish with a good attendance of " young people " both at Communion and at Evensong. Here at Portsea the attendance at Parish Communion and breakfast has grown from a mere handful of pioneers to an average of about 140 at the parish church and 90 at St. Wilfrid's. It can certainly be said that both have come to stay, and are more and more appreciated.

Now may I try to describe the 9.30 Celebration at the *parish church*, which as vicar I naturally know best. The bell rings from 9.15 to 9.25, and then stops; and we make every effort, not with unvarying success, to get people into the church before the service starts, so that they can quieten their minds and prepare themselves to worship. To help them we have our own simple and beautiful Communicants' Manual, which is given to candidates at Confirmation. Other copies are provided for the general congregation, though they are encouraged to buy their own from the Church bookstall. This Manual is printed privately for our own parochial use, and was prepared by Canon Southam, and revised by Canon Lunt. It contains helps to preparation and thanksgiving and meditation, instructions as to the service, and suggestions for prayer. The congregation, young and old, is mainly communicant, though we welcome the Sunday School children before Confirmation when they reach the Catechism Department. A few people value it as a service of worship without Communion at the time, having made their Communion at an earlier hour.

The celebrant normally takes the whole service, reading both Epistle and Gospel, and giving the short meditation. We follow the 1662 Office, with a few modifications. For example, we use our Lord's summary of the Commandments, split into two; we omit the Collect for the King, and adapt the last paragraph of the Prayer for the Church so as to include the Prayer for the Departed after the model of the proposed Prayer Book of 1928. We stand from the Sursum Corda to the end of the Benedictus, which is sung after the Sanctus. We substitute E.H. 335, "Wherefore, O Father," for the Agnus Dei; it is sung during the servers' communion and while the other administrants are receiving the paten and chalices. Complete silence is kept during the celebrant's act of communion—a most valuable feature. Our most striking addition is the closing prayers. During the last verses of the Ablutions hymn, the celebrant, preceded by crucifer, cantors, servers and clergy, comes down into the nave, and a simple prayer from the Manual is said all together by priest and people, followed by the mutual salutation, and

℣. Let us depart in peace:
℟. In the Name of the Lord.
℣. May the souls of all the faithful departed through the mercy of God rest in peace.

And we end with what to me is a very beautiful adaptation of the prayer of St. Richard of Chichester:

> " Dear Lord, of Thee three things I pray,
>   To know Thee more clearly,
>   To love Thee more dearly,
>   To follow more nearly,
>   —Day by day."

This is sung softly, the congregation kneeling, and the sight of young and old making this final act of dedication and resolve is most moving.

As to vesture, the celebrant wears plain linen vestments on ordinary Sundays, and a silk chasuble, amice and maniple on the great festivals.

The " ceremonial " is quite simple and dignified, with no frills. For the Meditation the celebrant does not go to the pulpit or remove his chasuble, but comes with his servers to the chancel steps. It is not an elaborate sermon, but either a simple devotional meditation or a plain instruction, giving the teaching of the day; it is often based on Collect, Epistle or Gospel, or gives the combined message of the three. It is never longer than eight to ten minutes.

As to music, we sing the two Kyries, Creed, Sursum Corda, Sanctus, Benedictus and Gloria. We vary between Merbecke, a congregational setting of Bach's Chorales by McGowan, and settings by Geoffrey Shaw and Hilton Stewart. We do not ask our regular choir, which already sings at Mattins and Evensong, but have men cantors, whose function is merely to lead the singing of the congregation. For we aim at congregational singing with no elaboration, and we have occasional congregational practices to try to get as many of the congregation as possible to know the music and take their full share in the worship. We begin with an Introit hymn, and have a Gradual hymn, a hymn at the Offertory, a hymn during the Communion of the people, and a hymn at the Ablutions. We try to select hymns of which the tunes and words are familiar to all, and use the English Hymnal, supplemented by a selection of special hymns in our privately printed Manual. Our aim is joy, simplicity and reality.

Hymns are not given out, but the numbers are put on the board. We do not disturb our worship by "handing the bag or plate round." Many of our people are partners in the Duplex Freewill Offering Scheme, and put their envelopes, as the others do their coins, in an alms dish at the bottom of the nave, which is brought to the altar during the Offertory. This we find more seemly, and though at first we puzzled our visitors, we now set their minds at rest, and receive their offerings by putting a notice by the alms dish, " Please place your offerings here."

That is a description of our Sunday by Sunday People's Communion. But once a year we have in very truth a Parish Communion, on the occasion of our parish church Patronal Festival, which we keep on a Sunday near the Visitation of the B.V.M. (July 2nd). Then, though we still provide earlier and later Celebrations for those who cannot come to the Parish Communion, we bring all our communicants from all the churches in the parish to a Parish Communion at the parish church at 9 a.m. We have had over 500 for the last two years, and it is just glorious to see the main body of the great church full of eager communicants. At our Festival we use the same order of service, except that immediately after the act of communion we stand and sing E.H. 329, " Strengthen for service," which is both challenging and inspiring. On this great day we communicate the people at all of our three altars. The service is a wonderful experience of the worshipping body coming in joyful thanksgiving to receive the Bread which cometh down from Heaven.

We have communal breakfasts after the Sunday by Sunday Celebrations, both at the parish church and at St. Wilfrid's. These are held in our Church Institutes. Loving " Marthas " prepare our simple breakfast, and, what is even more praiseworthy, wash up afterwards ! It is a very simple meal of tea, bread and butter and marmalade, for which we cheerfully pay threepence, or less in the case of the Catechism children. It is a scene of Christian fellowship and hilarity. Newcomers are here introduced to the family, and old friends come back to it, when they revisit the parish. There are no long faces. Everyone is happy in the family. Everyone talks, if they do not shout, but no one minds ! How can they help being joyful when " they have been with Jesus," and many of them are going off immediately after to devoted service of God's children as Sunday School teachers ? I am sure the parish breakfast is an integral part of this Liturgical movement. It is putting the Agape in its right place. Those who once come to it, never forsake it. In all this I have described the Communion and breakfast at the parish church, because I happen to be more familiar with it. But it is just the same at St. Wilfrid's, a very little more ornate in ceremonial, but in essence the same worshipful service, and the same joyous fellowship. Both churches are alike in finding a unique significance in the service.

So far we have been occupied mainly with description. Now for an attempted assessment of the value to us of a Parochial Communion and breakfast, as tested by our experience of fifteen years. I will begin with a rather profound observation made to me a short time ago. My friend said that you hear, especially from the young, all sorts of criticisms, often very unjust, against other Church services, especially Mattins and Evensong. Sermons are dull; hymns are bad; the Church is asleep, and so forth. But whether they attend it or not, no one criticises the Service of Holy Communion. Some things are too big and too sacred for the criticism even of the flippant. This leads us to try to make clear in what lies the outstanding value of the Parish Communion and breakfast. Let us work upwards and begin with some minor advantages.

1. It enables people, especially young people, who work hard and play hard during the week, and especially on Saturday, to have just that extra rest on Sunday morning which their nature needs. This I am sure is important to a generation which is witnessing a general " speed-up " of life in all directions.

2. The hour of 9.30 a.m. enables the young to have real corporate worship, and then, without putting God in the second place, to get out into the surrounding country, which is so refreshing to city-dwellers, and still be able to return home in time to worship God again in church at Evensong.

3. Young people who too often to-day are the only church-goers in a household can attend at 9.30 a.m. without unduly disturbing the older members of the family, and so antagonising them. This is a not unimportant point to young people who are often tempted to give up attendance at an *early* service because it involves inconveniencing their parents. The parish breakfast solves for them the problem of food, without worrying their households.

4. The old-established " hot Sunday dinner " in the middle of the day is still a tradition in many of

our homes. And, as communion and breakfast are all finished soon after 11 a.m., " Mother " can reach home in time to prepare the mid-day meal.

All these practical points are important in a mainly working-class parish, with a considerable number of young people. But we will turn to the more fundamental values to be found in our system.

A. *It combines fellowship in worship with a meal of fellowship*. This is vital. One of the problems of to-day, as one of the writers in *The Parish Communion* puts it, is to make the Church not a mere body of worshippers, but a worshipping body. This can be done to an increasing degree by patient effort. So think first of the *fellowship in worship*. Our 9.30 service gives a feeling of real corporateness. The individual is not swamped. But he feels himself a member of the worshipping body, with his own specific contribution of praise and prayer to bring to the larger whole. The communicants are not a chance aggregation, but a congregation. They sit all together, not, as sometimes at an 8 a.m. Celebration, removed as far as possible from each other, like islands in the Pacific Ocean! They form a group, a family, a body of Christ worshipping together the Risen, Ascended Lord. And this worship is focused on the common reception of the One Body and One Blood of the family's Heavenly Head. It is this that welds the family together. We do not only adore our Lord, great as this is; we humbly receive in faith with thanksgiving the Life which He gives. Here is true fellowship of worship based on communion with our Lord in His own service.

But this fellowship of worship needs its expression in

life, and finds this in the communal breakfast. Here those who have been made one body by common worship and common receiving of our Lord's life-giving Gift, express their corporate sense, their family spirit, by partaking together of earthly food in joy and fellowship. Eating together is a very social act, and a cup of tea, odd as this may sound, is good cement for friendship! At the parish breakfast is a happy family, in which the lonely may find friends ready to welcome them. Fellowship becomes a happy and a living thing. Class distinctions do not count for anything: all are members of the one family. Young and old meet on a common basis. We often talk here of our " Portsea family." It is generally admitted that its focus is the " 9.30 " with its handmaid, the breakfast.

B. *Such a service and breakfast as we have are suited for all schools of thought in the Church.* They are based on common essentials in which we agree. We have many shades of opinion in our congregations. But all can meet in fellowship, first at the Lord's Table, and then round the trestle tables of our Institute, and be the better for so meeting. We do not all fast before our communion, but we make it possible for those whose consciences bid them do so, to come to their communion and then take their first meal of the day at the subsequent breakfast. What is more, they walk considerable distances, as the buses are not usually running at that hour.

C. *Our Parish Communions and breakfasts produce a spirit of service.* Many of those who come and eat a hasty breakfast with us, go straight from it to the glorious and important privilege of " feeding Christ's lambs."

Stimulated by the experience of common worship and common meal, they give out what they have received in the service of God's children. They are the backbone of our parish life, unsparing in their devotion. I salute their self-sacrificing zeal. They prove that real religion will, if given the opportunity, issue in selfless service. They renew their strength week by week by waiting upon the Lord in communion.

D. *They produce a spirit of witness.* The experience which our people share among themselves fills many of them with a desire that others should share it. On Good Friday for the past two years we have had two Processions of Witness round as many of our streets as possible, culminating in a great Service of Witness conducted by our Bishop. For this service we have sent a personal invitation from the Bishop and myself to every one of our 9000 houses. Many of those who carry round these invitations and deliver them personally are drawn from those who have learned at our Parochial Communions and breakfasts what Christian worship and Christian fellowship are, and eagerly desire others to share this knowledge.

E. It gives us something real and definite, with which we link up the newly confirmed, and to which we invite the outsider, who very often is a lapsed communicant. Clubs have their value: we have many in Portsea, doing useful work. But if you can introduce your newly confirmed or bring back a lapsed communicant into the weekly " 9.30 " and persuade him to come to the breakfast afterwards, then, under God, you offer him something which has the capacity to hold him, because it satisfies his deepest needs. People are often lonely, especially in great cities.

They come to fresh work in a new place, and too often they do not tell their vicar, so that he cannot commend them on to one who will welcome them. But to those who are commended to us, or whom we discover, we can say without any hesitation, " Come to our 9.30 a.m., and come across to breakfast afterwards, and we guarantee you will meet people eager to be your friends." If they come, they stay.

F. I think it can be said that our Parish Communions and breakfasts tend to strengthen the habit of weekly and also week-day communion. It challenges our communicants to an ideal higher than the " once-a-month," and still more than the " three-times-a-year " convention which still lingers. It helps them to realise that God intends our communion to be regular Food rather than an occasional drug, and that, provided frequency never breeds formality, you can never come too often to the Table of the Lord.

I hope I do not write in too optimistic a vein. But my experience at Barking, where there is a Parish Communion at 9 a.m. not followed by breakfast, and at Portsea, makes me an enthusiastic advocate of what I am sure is a most promising movement in the Church. I have not dealt with the theology underlying this movement, except by inference. That has been adequately set forth in the larger book on the Parish Communion edited by Father Hebert. But I speak from a very happy experience of the practical value of this movement. Of course we have our problems, our ups and downs, our disappointments. We are not content with our numbers at 9.30. They are good, but not good enough. Our congregation at Mattins is naturally comparatively small; you cannot have it both ways! But I am sure we are on the right lines of progress! Worship and communion happily united, and followed by the fellowship of a common meal. And to build up a real communicant life, which issues in service, is to build something which is capable of growth. May I add that we are not " oncers," but have a very fine congregation at Evensong!

Of course the Parish Communion and breakfast are not a ready-made panacea, to be applied with the complacent words, " Well, that's that." It needs careful preliminary teaching before the experiment is made. It needs enthusiastic support afterwards both from clergy and Church officers. But the movement has life—" the life that is life indeed "—within itself, and under God's good hand it will go from strength to strength.

8

"THE FRUIT OF THE SPIRIT IS JOY"

By C. E. Goshawk

THE heart of the Christian religion is most clearly revealed in the worship of the Christian community. The religion of Jesus Christ is not primarily a system of philosophy or a code of moral laws, but a certain quality and manner of life—" the Way " it is called in the Acts—and that life is a life of worship, of loving and adoring response on the part of man to the love of the God who is his Creator, Redeemer and Sanctifier. Thus the services of the Christian Church are much more than meetings for spiritual guidance and inspiration: they are the necessary expression in praise, thanksgiving, penitence, and supplication, of the very life which makes the Christian community what it is. For this reason the type and arrangement of the services which are held in our churches can never be a matter of indifference; for they will manifest more or less unmistakably the health or otherwise of the unseen spiritual life of the congregation from which they flow. In turn that life will be modified for good or evil by the kind of services, and the manner of their performance, customary in that congregation.

If we look round at the Church of England as we

see it to-day, we find that, broadly speaking, the morning worship of the majority of parishes falls into one of two classes. There is first of all the church where the principal morning service is Morning Prayer, sung, with a choir present, and followed by a sermon and sometimes the Litany or a said celebration of Holy Communion. Secondly there is the church where the principal service is a sung Eucharist, with varying degrees of ceremonial elaboration, and with either none of the people communicating with the priest or at most a handful of elderly folk, representing only a small minority of those present. Neither of these arrangements can be considered satisfactory, for neither expresses adequately the true inner life of the Church. The office of Morning Prayer, beautiful and significant as it is, can never be the heart of Christian worship, which from the first has been in fulfilling the Lord's command " Do this " in the Eucharist. On the other hand, the solemn celebration with few or no communicants beside the priest, though much nearer to the mind of the Church through the ages, which we believe to be the mind of Christ, yet fails to set forth the whole of the meaning of the Lord's service, in which the communion of the people— " Drink ye *all* of this "—is not an optional addition to the essential rite, but an integral and necessary part of it.

Of recent years there has been a growing realisation of these truths amongst the clergy and faithful laity, and in consequence a widespread interest in a third possible arrangement of the morning service, and its actual adoption in many places. This is the arrangement for which this book pleads—namely, the solemn celebration of the Holy Eucharist at an hour late enough to make possible the gathering together of the majority of the people, and still early enough for them to make their communion fasting. In practice it is found that round about 9 o'clock is such an hour.

The writer first came across this service in 1923 at the parish church of Yarm-on-Tees, Yorkshire. A parochial mission had lately been held in this parish, and one of the results of the quickening of spiritual life by the mission had been the starting of a " Parish Eucharist " at 9 o'clock every Sunday, followed by a communal breakfast in the adjoining parish hall. This has continued without a break, I believe, up to the present time. No doubt in those fourteen years the arrangement has been thoroughly tested.

A month's experience in this parish created in me such a deep impression of the fellowship in worship which seemed to have grown up round that service that when, in 1925, I was given charge of the Church of the Ascension, a district church in the parish of Malvern Link, Worcestershire, the same plan was adopted there. For some time previously the only morning service had been a sung Eucharist at 8 o'clock, after which the people were supposed to go down to the parish church for the 11 o'clock service there. The great drawback to the early hour of 8 was that the older people—in what is called a " residential " district—found it difficult to attend, and it was almost impossible to get the children. The hour of the Eucharist was therefore changed to 9 and a parish breakfast afterwards was begun. Four years' experience of this plan showed, as later experience confirmed, that no spectacular growth of the congregation in mere

H

numbers is to be looked for by the establishment of this service, but that what does clearly grow under its influence is a certain " atmosphere," a quality or spirit among the loyal nucleus who become regular attendants. Of this " atmosphere " more will be said later.

Then in 1932 the writer came to his present parish, a new parish with a newly consecrated parish church, in a solidly working-class neighbourhood. Here the problem of Sunday services was somewhat different. The tradition for some years had been a High Mass (the name accepted and used by all), at which nobody was expected to, or ever did, communicate beside the priest. Communion was received at Low Mass at 8 and 9.30. For reasons which this book should help to make clear, this was felt to be unsatisfactory, and so, after these reasons had been carefully explained, both from the pulpit and in the Parish Magazine, the following Sunday morning services were substituted: Low Mass at 8, High Mass with general communion at 9.30. The hour of 9.30 was chosen for the Parish Mass, rather than the ideally preferable hour of 9, because the parish had been accustomed to a Mass at this time, and the change of habit involved was thus lessened. It has so far been found impracticable to hold a parish breakfast every Sunday, although we have one from time to time on such week-days as Ascension Day. But tea and biscuits are available in the parish hall after Mass, and a few people take this refreshment, and others stay on with them for friendly intercourse. Thus we have at any rate some of the features of the parish breakfast.

Something may be said about the actual rendering

of the Mass. Children are present, and receive the
Faith Press Gospel stamps for regular attendance.
The choir is, of course, present, and the music is
almost invariably that of Merbecke, which everyone
knows and sings heartily. With an assistant priest
normally on the staff, and a loyal and intelligent
layman to act as sub-deacon or epistoler, the liturgy
is rendered with the full ceremonial of High Mass,
modified in some particulars to accord with the Church
of England rite. A procession precedes the Mass on
the great festivals, and in Lent the Litany is sung in
this way. Fasting communion is taught, expected,
and, to the best of my knowledge, practised by our
people. The greater part of the confirmed members
of the congregation present receive Holy Communion.
A short sermon is always preached, and in spite of this
we come out of church at 10.30, except when there is a
procession, and complaints as to the length of the
service are seldom heard. We try to make the sermon
instructional and liturgical—that is, explanatory of
the Collect, Epistle or Gospel for the day, or of some
feature in the rite or its accompanying ceremonial.
In this way the sermon is saved from becoming an
isolated and detached element in the service with
little or no bearing on the purpose for which we are
gathered together.

In the past five years various difficulties have, of
course, presented themselves, some of them likely to
appear in any parish, and others probably due to the
particular circumstances here. There has not been
any remarkable increase in the congregation, though
it has been difficult to make any satisfactory estimate,
owing to the migration of many of our folk during the

years of the depression to seek work elsewhere. It should be understood, I think, that a parish which adopted this plan expecting thereby to draw larger congregations is likely to be disappointed with the results. These are of a less obvious nature, though no less real and valuable on that account. We will attempt to analyse them in a moment. Meanwhile it may be useful to consider the difficulties which must be faced. In the first place there is in most parishes a number of people who resent changes of any sort, especially any change in the accustomed hour of services. Then there are those who dislike making their communion at a sung service; some cannot, or are unwilling to, fast till 10 or 10.30; some are distracted by the presence of the children at Mass; some do not feel the Sunday has been properly kept unless they have been to church between breakfast and dinner. All these can only be dealt with by patient and repeated explanation of the reasons underlying the changes. Much can be done in this way when there is mutual trust and respect between priest and people. But we must be prepared in the last resort to fail to win them over; this is part of the penalty which must be paid for any change in the customs of a parish. Whether it is worth while must, of course, be thoroughly weighed beforehand.

Then, again, not all parents will put themselves out to see that the children are ready for church at this hour. In a working-class parish such as this the prevailing habit is against early rising on Sunday, and we have not yet solved the problem of how to get the children to Mass in anything like the numbers that they come to afternoon Sunday School. But this draw-

back is outweighed, in my opinion, by the great
advantage of familiarising those who do come with a
service at which they see their elder brothers and sisters
—indeed, people of all ages—going up to the altar to
make their communion.   The beneficial effects of this
are realised at the time of preparation for Confirmation and First Communion.   The late Sunday rising
is also an obstacle to be overcome in the case of communicants—the young people, especially, do not find
it easy to go against the family habits in this matter.
But this is equally so where the Mass with Communion is at 8 o'clock.   Indeed, when we exhort
them to come at 9 or 9.30 we are meeting them, as it
were, halfway, and not entirely ignoring the reasonable
desire of a worker, who has to get up early all the
week, for a little extra sleep on Sunday.   But ultimately, of course, some sacrifice and self-discipline
are called for in either case.   It is well that it should
be so, and a sifting of the keen from the half-hearted
will always be made by this question of communion.
Where there is an 11 o'clock service in a working-class
parish there may be a larger congregation, but there
is a danger that the late risers may satisfy their conscience by attendance at this service only, for which
little real discipline is required.

As to the parish breakfast, there are two difficulties
in a poor parish.   The first is that of expense.   A
fixed charge is apt to deter many from staying to
breakfast, while a collection has been found not always
to cover the cost (we have tried it on such occasions
as Ascension Day).   Again, the Sunday breakfast
is in many of our homes the one substantial breakfast
of the week, and healthy young men and women

cannot be expected to forgo it for a light meal of sandwiches and buns. The compromise we have adopted is certainly not ideal, but has been found to be accompanied by at least some of the desirable features of the parish breakfast proper.

Let us now turn to the results of the adoption of this plan as they have been found by the writer in the three parishes in which he has had personal experience of its working. They are all intangible—that is to say not the kind of results the "practical" man asks for, results which can be tabulated and counted. They are rather spiritual results, not strikingly obvious to a casual observer, but real and unmistakable to one who is alert to recognise the Holy Spirit's working.

The first I should call the *development of the family spirit* in the congregation—a new conception of unity and fellowship. Ideally this belongs to the Church as such, whatever form its services may take. But in actual experience we find many congregations which show little signs of that fellowship (*Koinonia*) and brotherly love (*Philadelphia*) which marked the apostolic days. But with the establishment of the Parish Mass and breakfast there has been a steady growth of corporate life amongst us. We are few in numbers, but we are learning steadily the meaning of our weekly Communion together (fellowship in spiritual things) and common breakfast (fellowship in material things). Moreover, the family spirit is encouraged by the actual presence at Mass of families as such—father, mother and children, in some cases. Old people and newly confirmed children, youths and maidens, the employer (we have one in our congregation) and employed, kneel side by side at the altar of God, and afterwards share

the friendly cup of tea. Occasionally we have had an
Indian Christian staying with us and vividly demon-
strating, as he knelt at the altar with us, that the
Bread of life received there truly makes us " one bread,
one body." I believe that this spirit of fellowship has
been powerfully assisted, too, by the fact that in some
cases our people have deliberately put aside their own
preference in the matter of the hour of service, and
joined with us at some inconvenience to themselves,
out of loyalty to the family life of the parish. Unity
can only come when the individual sinks himself in
the life of the Body, and in so far as the Parish Mass
calls for such self-effacement from many who would
personally be more at home at an 8 or 11 o'clock
Mass, it is providing a fertile soil for the growth of the
spirit of unity.

The second result I would name springs from this
unity and is a manifestation of it—namely, the development of *really congregational worship*; and by congregational worship I mean an offering of praise, penitence,
thanksgiving and supplication in which the whole body
of the faithful plays a real and active, not merely a
passive, part. We all know the congregation which
seems to look upon the clergy and choir as there to
perform a certain ceremony at which the layfolk
look on more or less approvingly, but without com-
mitting themselves to a share in it—the congregation
which makes no responses at a said service and stands
obstinately dumb at a choral one. It is my firm
belief that the Parish Mass lifts the people out of this
unchristian attitude towards the worship of the Church
as nothing else can. This development is furthered
in our case by the situation of the organ and choir

in a gallery at the west end of the church, where their music seems to support and encourage the singing of the people, rather than to drag it unwillingly forward, or even to frown it down as an impertinence, as so often seems to be the case where the musicians come between the people and the altar. Be that as it may, the adoption of a simple and invariable setting of the liturgical text, such as Merbecke's, is undoubtedly the way to make possible an answer to the prayer " O Lord, open thou our lips, and our mouth shall show forth thy praise." Then again, the short instructional sermon gives the opportunity to explain the importance of the people's Amens and other responses, to suggest special " intentions " of a corporate nature, to awaken interest in the symbolism of the sanctuary and the significance of ceremonial, so that the congregation comes to take an intelligent interest in what is going on—the first stage towards active co-operation. Above all, the drama of the liturgy moves forward week by week to its consummation in the Communion of the people, the best and most complete form of their co-operation in the offering of the Sacrifice, from which they are so often debarred at an 11 o'clock Mass. Though many of our simple folk might be unable to put their feelings into words, I am confident that they are growing to understand more and more that they come to church to *do* something, and not merely to look on.

Thirdly, there is a spirit at the Parish Mass, very difficult to describe, but for which the best name perhaps is *joyfulness*. It is not just the " heartiness " of a service at which people " make a cheerful noise unto the God of Jacob ": it is not that complacent

and irritating cheerfulness which is sometimes found
in Church people whose religion does not go very deep;
nor is it that militant rejoicing in the Catholic Faith
which sometimes shows itself in a contemptuous attitude towards those Christians whose way of worship
is not ours. It is associated, in my mind at least, with
the sense of our Lord's living presence in our midst,
just as the infant Church experienced it after Pentecost:
" I will see you again and your heart shall rejoice and
your joy no man taketh from you." Over the High
Altar of our church is a magnificent figure of the
Risen Christ, crowned and vested as Priest, "reigning
from the Tree." Whether or not under the influence
of this Figure, rather than that of the crucifix more
common in our churches, there certainly is at the
Parish Mass a true feeling of Easter victory and
Easter joy. Not that the Passion is not preached, or
understood by our people, but that at the Breaking
of Bread we seem to have passed beyond Calvary to
the great Forty Days, and as the Kiss of Peace passes
from minister to minister in the sanctuary, with its
accompanying salutation, " The peace of the Lord
be always with you," we hear the Lord's " Peace be
unto you," and eagerly crowd round Him at our
communion to behold the scarred Hands and the riven
Side. Perhaps this sounds fanciful; but, then, the
deepest things of the spirit cannot be pressed into the
unyielding mould of sober prose. If joyfulness is the
right word for what has been described, who will undertake to define it in the cold language of philosophy?

Certain it is that when one of our " littlest ones "
runs out of his seat during Mass, we can smile without
self-consciousness, for we remember, " Suffer the little

children to come unto Me ": when one of our elderly
rheumatic folk stands up beside the kneeling figures
at the communion rail to receive the Body which
will "preserve" that poor body "unto everlasting
life," we believe that "the power of the Lord" is
"present to heal"; when some busy mother hurries
straight from the altar to get the family dinner, we
do not think she is hardly judged by Him who "loved
Martha" as well as her sister Mary. It is all "homely,"
as our folk say, it is all very real and meaningful—not a
dull routine performance; and that because the Lord
is "made known unto us in the breaking of bread,"
because we have lifted up our hearts unto the Lord,
and our hearts rejoice, and our joy no man taketh
from us.

WHERE TOWN AND COUNTRY MEET

By B. P. Robin

" Things which are seen were not made of things which do appear," and Parish Communions and Breakfasts, like everything else, have their beginnings in the realm of the spirit, in the spheres of faith and thought.

If, then, this is to be an account of my personal experience of the Parish Communion and Breakfast in the parish which I serve, I must begin where it began, with the thoughts and convictions which led me, and then our people with me, to inaugurate it.

All through the twenty-five years of my ministry I had grown steadily to the conviction that as worship— the communion of man with the Eternal Spirit—is obviously the highest activity of man, so corporate worship is the highest kind of worship, and the Holy Communion the highest kind of corporate worship. " The chief end of man is to glorify God and enjoy Him for ever," and that is attained by men in proportion as they are wholly and fully alive in every part of their being. But life is impossible in isolation. It can only come to its full richness and glory when it is in touch with all life at all points, both giving fully

and receiving fully, each life a sort of " exchange and
mart," out of and into and through which are constantly pouring all the currents of all life. For such a
fulness of life, communion with God, the Source of
all life, is obviously essential. What we do not always
see is that communion with all other life—the life of
men and indeed of the whole creation—is an essential
also.

It is the vision of such an unimagined richness of
individual and corporate life in body, mind and spirit,
that again and again sweeps St. Paul off his feet in
his letters to the young Christian communities to
whom he is trying to show " the riches of the glory of
the inheritance " of life in Christ. And as one grows
year by year in the unending discovery of what it was
Christ gave us when He said so simply, " Do this in
remembrance of Me," one finds that in the Holy
Communion—and there alone—is summed up and
expressed and achieved " the riches of the glory of
the inheritance." Here is life at the full. First,
God's initial gift of life to us through our creation
and redemption, calling and enabling us to the response of worship. Then the giving by each worshipper of all that he is and has into the great harmony
of consciously corporate worship that rises from the
whole worshipping body to God. Then the great
surging rhythm of the Trisagion, in which the little
local body of worshippers knows itself caught up and
" tuned in " to the rhythmic worshipping response of
all creation to the Creator—not only " with angels
and archangels and all the company of heaven," but
also with the surge of the world's seas, the swing of
tides, the ordered movement of the stars, the flight of

birds, and " every created thing." The unresting, inarticulate Trisagion of all the Universe is made articulate in the " Holy, Holy, Holy " of each local Eucharist. Then, in the Consecration and Oblation, we, conscious now of our unity as Christ's mystical Body, are taken up above our " space–time " limitations into His perpetual oblation of Himself, and united with Him, offered by Him, made acceptable in Him, to the Father. And last—the Communion— the Receiving which is the essential and inseparable climax of the Offering, and in which " the Prince of life " turns to renew in His mystical Body His own " princely " life. It is to the Body that He gives that life, and each worshipper is able to receive it because he is, and just in so far as he truly and fully is, a member of the Body. The single worshipper can find the fullness of life, the fullness of his own individuality, only as a member of the true and literal " in-divid-uality " of that Body of Christ in which God's " elect "—the company of the redeemed—are " knit together in one communion and fellowship."

Well, it is the growth of such convictions and discoveries as these which I have here tried very shortly and inadequately to summarise, that has led me to three strong convictions about the matter we are discussing.

The first is shared nowadays, I believe, by the very great majority of Christians, even in our own country, and by many in the " Free Churches." It is that there is no other way of worship which can come anywhere near to competing with the Holy Communion as the heart and hallmark of a " Christian " Sunday. A living obedience to our Lord's command has proved this in the spiritual experience of all Christendom in all ages.

My second conviction, not perhaps so widely shared, but backed both by the widespread " Liturgical Reform " movement in the Roman Church and by the convictions of Evangelical Christians everywhere, is that the introduction and encouragement of a non-communicating Eucharist was one of the few mistakes of the Catholic Revival. The restoration of the Holy Eucharist to the central place in Sunday worship must be the restoration of a Communion.

My third conviction is that—because such a Communion must be early enough to be " the first food of the day," and late enough to be a " central " service, and even more because of the enormous value of a social and secular expression of the " communion and fellowship " which have just been recreated at the altar—a " Communion Breakfast " is, not indeed an essential, but quite literally a " consummation devoutly to be desired." It is indeed in our experience in this parish, far more than I had dreamed it could be, a " consummation " of the Eucharistic worship and Communion.

This conviction, by comparison with the others, is shared, I know, by only a small body as yet. But the discovery of the value and happiness of such a breakfast will astonish those who are bold enough to try it.

That, then, in brief, is the spiritual history and foundation of the Parish Communion and Breakfast as it has come into being in this parish. Let me turn now to what are called " practical " details, pausing only to give what should be an unnecessary warning—that without such a spiritual history and abiding foundation the institution of a Parish Communion and Breakfast as "the right thing" would make it only one more of those "stunts" which can do nothing but destroy the spiritual life of any community.

The Character of the Parish

Those who may read this essay will like to know what kind of parish this is, as a basis for comparison with their own.

It *was* just a large country parish of about twelve square miles, with a population of 1100, the church lying about four miles from Birkenhead, beyond which, just across the Mersey, is Liverpool. During the last few years, however, there has been much new building in the suburbs of Birkenhead, which has spread over the parish boundary and brought about 700 houses—mainly of clerks and artisans from both Birkenhead and Liverpool—into the parish. In two other parts of the parish there has also been considerable building of small houses. None of this new building is within one and a half miles of the parish church (the only church building in the parish), which stands in a hamlet of a dozen houses, surrounded still by "country." Because of this "country" character—rare about here—and of a certain beauty of simplicity which marks the church and which we try to preserve in its services, the church draws a certain number of people from various parts of the surrounding district. The great bulk of our congregation thus comes anything from one to four miles to church.

These conditions, you may say, provide a ready-made " excuse " for a Communion breakfast simply on the ground of its convenience. But to anyone coming to the breakfast it would be immediately clear that those who come, continue to come because they find in it something very much more than a convenience.

Preparing the Ground

Clergy sometimes complain that their people take little interest in, and show little sense of responsibility for, the services of their parish church. I cannot help thinking that this is very often the fault of the priest, whose attitude about the church and all that is done in it is quite often and quite obviously that it is " my," and not " our " church. Personally I think it is both wrong and stupid of a priest to make radical alterations in the services of a church as soon as he takes charge, however right in themselves such changes may be. If he will by patience and consideration set himself to win his people's trust, they will follow him further in five years than he would be able to drive them in ten.

Acting on this principle, I tried here for four years to teach the Faith, without altering in any way the Sunday services, which were Holy Communion at 8 a.m. and Mattins and Sermon at 10.30. Even then we did not change, but only added to, the existing services. I told my excellent P.C.C. that I proposed to add a second Eucharist—to be sung by the congregation—between the present services. They agreed unanimously, only protesting that I was giving myself more work.

I then used the Wednesday evening services in Lent (1935) for a series of careful instructions on " The Art and Practice of Worship," dealing with the Eucharist on doctrinal, devotional and practical grounds.

Since this was to be essentially the Offering " of the people by the people," *i.e.* a sung but not a choral Eucharist, I suggested that those who would should stay behind after each Wednesday service to learn and practise the music of the liturgy. The whole congregation of fifty or sixty stayed each week with hardly ever an exception.

The musical setting which I chose, in consultation with my very able choirmaster, was Dr. Sydney H. Nicholson's Communion Service in C. For a congregation hardly any of whom would have known even the meaning of the word " Plainsong," this provided a simple, dignified and tuneful setting which all could appreciate. In commending a new kind of service to people, the choice of music is important. We have used this setting—and no other—for two and a half years, and it has " worn " very well indeed. I inquire from time to time whether people are feeling tired of it, and always get an enthusiastic negative. The parts we sing are—the " 10th " Kyrie (we use our Lord's summary of the Decalogue at this service), the Gloria and Thanks at the Gospel, the Sursum Corda, Preface, Sanctus, Benedictus, Agnus and Gloria, with five hymns in the usual places.

People are beginning to tell me now that a hymn of any length during the people's communion does not leave them time for all that they want to do during that interval in the way of oblation, thanks-

I

giving and intercession. I reply, " Well, not everyone has got as far as that yet. Many still need a
hymn, and grown-ups must keep step with children."
But as we all grow, I daresay we shall come to drop
the " communion " hymn.

Having thus prepared the ground as well as I could
before and during Lent, I decided that though Easter
Day was the obvious day to " launch " the Parish
Communion, the crowd of rather irregular and half-
instructed communicants that, sad to say, characterises
Easter Day in most parishes, would be a wrong environment for such a new venture. So we sang our
first Parish Communion on Low Sunday, 1935.

The Hour of Service

This question—a possibly difficult one in some
parishes—was very simply settled for us by the fact
that the Parish Communion and breakfast had to be
fitted in between 8.45 and 10.30. We chose 9 a.m.
because either earlier or later was impossible. We
have since put Mattins at 10.45, to give a little more
time, but even if we had had a choice, I think we
should have chosen 9, or at the latest 9.15.

Several factors govern the choice of the hour. Two
of them I have already mentioned :—

(*a*) That the service, being essentially a Communion
as well as a Eucharist, should be early enough to make
a " fasting communion " natural and practicable.

(*b*) That it should be late enough to allow of its
taking its place as the central service. Let me add—

(*c*) That in these days of speed and strain, when many
young people set out for their work at 6.30 a.m. and
(with night school) may not finish till 10.30 p.m. on four

nights a week, it is not a concession to laziness, but an encouragement to needed rest, to arrange the Parish Communion later than 8 a.m.

But—(d) many working folk need to be able to get back home in time to get the mid-day dinner, so that a Parish Communion placed early enough may help to make possible a congregation of all " classes " and override the bad and prevalent class-division between Mattins and Evensong.

The last factor in the choice of the hour will be irrelevant in nice, compact parishes, but is a large consideration in a scattered one like ours.   It is—

(e) Transport. Some of our people have cars, and are very good at giving lifts to others. Some come on bicycles, but many, with two miles to do before breakfast, are dependent on buses. There are two bus services—the Birkenhead Corporation and the Crosville Co.—which pass within five minutes' walk of the church. But on Sundays the former service started just too late, and the latter much too late for our purpose. The Corporation, on being approached, kindly undertook to put their first bus five minutes earlier, thus getting people from that end of the parish to church just in time. To serve the other end, I charter each Sunday a Crosville bus, which can be hailed by anyone anywhere en route. Passengers put their fares into a box in the church on arrival. I pocket the proceeds and pay the Company, hoping for the day when the Company will run this bus as a part of their regular service.

This bus is known as " The Church Bus," and after it had been running regularly and unobtrusively for more than a year, the gentlemen of the Press

stumbled upon it, hailed it joyfully as " copy," and
" featured " it in headlines such as " THE RECTOR'S
BUS "—" Plan to lure church laggards "—" AND
BREAKFAST TOO!! " The next Sunday morning I
found three persevering youths with pendent cigar-
ettes and press cameras—one of them having travelled
fifty miles—waiting outside the church to " shoot "
the " Rector's bus." When I had pointed out that this
particular bit of " news " was already fifteen months
old, and that I did not want to have to put either
them or their cameras in the Rectory duckpond, they
went away and troubled us no more.

But, in passing, I believe there are wider possibilities
in the " church bus." Might it not be practicable for
country parishes with scattered hamlets and large
half-empty churches at the centre, instead of sinking
large sums in building mission churches (thereby too
often creating local cliques) and either adding to or
overworking the existing staff of clergy in order to
serve them, to invest in a " church bus," which would
lessen the work of the clergy, help to fill the parish
church, and have a unifying effect on the parish as a
whole?

The Breakfast : Its Purpose and its Management

(a) *Its Purpose.* First and foremost stands its spiritual
purpose and value, at which I have already hinted.
I hoped that it would help to overcome the disastrous
individualism which has characterised—and largely
sterilised—the spiritual life of the greater part of
Christendom for many centuries. Thousands of faithful communicants still regard what they call " my

communion " as a private affair between God and themselves.

I hoped that it would provide a channel through which week by week the spiritual " communion and fellowship " founded at the altar in the worship of the Father and the shared life of the Son might overflow as a " fellowship of the Holy Ghost " dynamic in the relationships of daily life, and that people would make friendships at the table which would lead to mutual service afterwards.

I hoped that newcomers to the parish would be urged to come to the Communion Breakfast and find a warm and immediate welcome into a living fellowship, instead of having to say—what one is always hearing—" I've been to that church for three years, and not a soul has ever spoken to me."

I hoped that the grace of the altar overflowing to the table would override the barriers of class and wealth and education.

I hoped that the fellowship begun at the Eucharist, and finding expression at the Breakfast, would react again to deepen the spirit of corporate worship at the Eucharist.

I hoped that thus by action and reaction there might be produced in this small corner of the Kingdom, in however small a way, a " working model," a microcosm of the world-wide Kingdom, a practical demonstration in miniature of the sheer common sense of God's plan for a commonwealth of men, an evangelistic witness which, by the clear reality of its divine and human fellowship, would commend itself to others and draw them in.

All these hopes may sound extravagant, but they

have not proved so. Not one of them but has been already in some degree fulfilled, some far more than I had imagined possible.

Besides these greater purposes, the breakfast has other simpler ones—*e.g.* to enable whole families to come together to the Eucharist, without having to leave someone behind to cook the breakfast, to enable maids and mistresses to come together and breakfast together, as they do, and to afford that much rest from Sunday household work.

(*b*) *Its Management*. The mere introduction of the idea of a Communal breakfast requires care. To the Englishman the Sunday family breakfast is almost as sacred an institution as the roast beef and apple tart of Sunday mid-day. He values it rightly and really as a family gathering, and his natural man resents the substitution of publicity for privacy at his breakfast. His resentment will remain until he sees the value, and experiences the fellowship, of the larger family gathering. In this parish we got over the unfamiliarity of the idea by having for two or three years previously an annual Communal breakfast as a welcome to the newly confirmed after their first Communion.

The breakfast itself is managed here by a committee of five women, which meets once a quarter These five deal with all its affairs. Each of them is responsible for the running of the breakfast on one Sunday in five, and for finding her own team of five helpers, except that we pay a woman one shilling and sixpence each Sunday for cooking and washing up.

We get our supplies at wholesale rates from a first-class firm, though the larder is sometimes enriched by gifts of home-made jam or marmalade. Our menu is—unlimited tea, bread, butter, jam and marmalade, and a meat course which on alternate Sundays is hot sausages, and on the others cold ham, tongue, brawn, etc., or boiled eggs. The price of breakfast is fourpence, the Committee keeps the most careful accounts, and we make a profit of about fourpence a Sunday, over a period. After breakfast any surplus food is bought in at cost price by those who can use it at home.

The problem of knowing how many to cater for with so small a financial margin we solved with fair success for the first year by posting a paper on the church door with pencil attached, asking people to put a pencil-stroke on the paper that Sunday if they intended to be at breakfast the *next* Sunday. Now that we have found by experience—though the numbers grow slowly all the time—about how many to expect on various Sundays, we still put our small framed notice on the door before the Parish Communion, so as to get the exact numbers, but only for the day itself.

For more than two years—we have only just got our Parish Hall—we had to clear the school desks every Saturday morning, carry trestle-tables, chairs, crockery, etc., a distance of 100 yards, and put everything back again early on Monday morning.

This and perhaps some other things I have mentioned may provide an answer to those who are inclined to say, of this as of other things, " Well, of course it is easy enough in some parishes, but it couldn't be done here." I would say that a big new venture is not easy anywhere, but it is possible in most places, given the vision and the will.

The breakfast has won its way as steadily as the

Parish Communion itself, and now practically everyone who comes to the Communion comes to breakfast too. The average number of communicants at the Parish Communion on ordinary Sundays two years ago was twenty-six, now it is forty-three. The number at 8 a.m. has remained almost as it was, with perhaps a slight increase.

In this parish, indeed, the Parish Communion and Breakfast (as a quite indivisible entity) has been the solution of several problems that confront most parishes. But though obviously it is as yet only in its infancy, it is already the creative, dynamic and evangelistic heart of the life of the parish. We have no " organisations " of any kind to " feed " it, no societies, guilds, unions, clubs or such to " draw people to church." I have stood for the principle that in any parish there is really only one society—the Holy, Catholic Church, as represented by the local congregation—and there is only one complete and perfect expression of all that the Church means, and it is the Holy Communion. There the divine organism, the Body of Christ, finds itself, expresses itself, fulfils itself. Thence it goes out—from the altar to the table—to find, express and fulfil its divine unity in the secular environment. Thence again it passes out into the world of daily life and work and contacts, to express and fulfil and declare that secret of life in fellowship which it has found, and to tell others where it is to be found, and bring them to the finding. " That which we have seen and heard declare we unto you, that ye also may have fellowship with us : and truly our fellowship is with the Father, and with his Son Jesus Christ."

UNITY OF SPIRIT IN A COUNTRY VILLAGE

By Kenneth G. Packard

We most humbly beseech Thee . . . to receive these our prayers which we offer unto Thy divine Majesty, beseeching Thee to inspire the universal Church with the spirit of truth, unity and concord.

Thus the great prayer for the Church in her warfare here on earth asks that the soldiers, who were enlisted in her service at their baptism, may be a truly united army. For the conflict is a grim one, against the principalities, the powers, the spiritual hosts of wickedness, and nothing is more certain to injure the cause than dissension, division, treachery in the ranks. More and more, thank God, it is coming home to us how "great dangers we are in by our unhappy divisions." These divisions, however, we commonly think of only in terms of the "reunion of Christendom," which forms the subject of the petition quoted at the head of this chapter.

There is another kind of unity, equally important, but often almost overlooked. This is the unity of the "local branch" of Christ's Church, of the parish or congregation; and when the Prayer for the Church continues " *and grant that all they that do confess Thy holy Name may agree in the truth of Thy holy Word and live in unity and godly love*," it is concerned that the Christians in each parish or unit of the Church may become what they are meant to be, a unity, a band of brothers and sisters in Christ Jesus, a family.

Yet there is an obvious lack of family-sense in our Church life : we see men and women coming together to the Father's house, the Father's table, yet hardly recognising each other away from it, still less treating each other as blood-relations; we find the congregation at an early celebration quite out of touch with the worshippers at Evensong in the same parish. The Church has, in fact, come to be regarded mainly as an institution for providing spiritual sustenance for individuals, instead of the home of the Christian family in each place, the centre of their spiritual unity with God and with each other.

The Church of Christ's soldiers militant here on earth praying for unity echoes the sacramental prayer of our Lord Himself, " that they may all be one, even as We are, that the world may know that thou hast sent Me "; it accords, too, with the teaching of the great apostle of the Gentiles. Few things emerge so clearly from a study of St. Paul's Epistles as a whole than that they are letters written to definite church-communities, and are concerned in the main with actual problems and situations which have arisen in the family life of each such community. When read in conjunction with the Acts, they make plain to us how Christianity, wherever it went, produced in each place where it took root this kind of closely-knit community, the members all intensely conscious of their family relationship to each other because of their relationship to the Father and the great Elder Brother. In such a church-community, as in a human family, each has his peculiar place, and his peculiar contribution to make. All this runs like a golden thread through the Epistles (and not only St. Paul's), finding its clearest expression in the great metaphor of the body and its parts or members, nowadays so familiar a way of speaking that we may easily fail to see how daring and striking it must have appeared to those who first heard it from St. Paul. For the Body as a whole, in St. Paul's language, is none other than the Lord Himself: each member is an integral part of the living Whole.

But it is not only in St. Paul's writings that this organic unity of the Church, as a whole and in its " local branches," is to be found. The same great conception lies at the heart of the teaching of the Lord Himself. There is the closest of parallels, for instance, between St. Paul's analogy of the body and its members and Christ's figure of the Vine and the branches. Nor is this to be found only in the Fourth Gospel; the Lord's Prayer, for instance, is essentially the prayer for the members of a family.[1]

This idea of the family character of the Church, which by many is coming to be recognised as the authentic pattern of Christianity as it came from the Founder's mould, was dimly taking shape in the writer's mind some years ago, but for a time he could find no satisfactory means of expressing it in the practical life of a parish. Considerable help in clarifying his thoughts

---

[1] This emerges all the more clearly when, as modern linguistic research has shown, we see that " Give us this day our daily bread " meant originally something very like " Give each of us his family share of the food."

came from contact with the Toc H movement. For
this society aims (often, alas! with tragic lack of fulfil-
ment in practice) [1] at "building a number of self-
supporting branches, comprising men of *every* social,
intellectual, vocational and religious type, who are
gradually to learn to live and work together as a
family." It is almost an exact picture of what the
Church, on one side of its life, is meant, according to
the New Testament, to be.

Meanwhile the writer, previously vicar of a large
industrial parish in the Midlands, found himself in
charge of a country parish of some six or seven hundred
souls in Sussex. It was an unusual type of country
parish, at least for the South of England, for almost the
entire population consisted of families on or near the
lowest wage-level, yet not (except for a very few) farm-
labourers. Many of the men were more or less casual
labourers, finding employment on road-works, or
under builders; others worked in the big chestnut
woods making stakes for "economic fencing"; others
again were employed in gardens, stables, houses
belonging to wealthy residents in the neighbourhood.
A great trunk road ran through the parish, bringing,
in summer, and especially on Sundays, an immense
stream of Londoners intent on seeking pleasure in the
quickest way, usually a liquid one! At the big cross-

[1] The failure of Toc H, in many places, to achieve anything
like this ideal, appears to be due to its so often leaving out in
practice the very keystone of the whole fabric—namely, a
conscious relationship to the Father, without whom there obviously
can be no real family at all.

This is not a condemnation of Toc H; it only means that Toc H
cannot be, and usually recognises that it cannot be, a *substitute*
for the Church, though, if it is alive to its opportunities, it can contribute to the realisation of the Christian family in the parish.

roads in the village, it was common to see as many as forty charabancs outside the " pub " on a Sunday. This impact of the London holiday-maker, in his least responsible mood, on the village had the effect of a kind of superficial urbanisation, the villager picking up some of the less desirable features of town life, and, needless to say, had a disastrous effect upon many of the youth of the parish.

If the church had been built where the " pub " was, things might have been very different, but actually the situation of the parish church (like that of the school, the vicarage, and village hall) was half a mile from this. It is not a matter for wonder that few of the villagers, very few indeed of those from the poorer side of the parish, found their way with any regularity to the House of God.

And what of the parish church itself—what of the worship and the Church life?

It was a particularly lovely church, lavishly adorned by the squire and his wife in memory of an only son, a victim of the Great War. For many years there had been more of a Catholic tradition than in the neighbouring parishes, vestments had been in use since 1915, and there was a children's sung Eucharist on Sundays. This latter was well attended by the Sunday Schools, but by hardly any one else, and, with the rarest exceptions, none of the children ever " stuck " after leaving day-school.

Such was the condition of things when, in June 1936, a parochial mission was held in the village; and lasted for over a fortnight (three Sundays). This mission marked a turning-point for the Church in the parish. Not that anything very sensational happened; but it meant new beginnings, beginnings which were big with promise for the future, and especially in the direction of local unity, that " Christian family-sense " of which we have spoken.

Of these new beginnings the most important was the Parish Communion, celebrated each Sunday at 9 a.m., and followed by a homely meal in a room conveniently near the church. It was not without great misgivings that the incumbent, with whom of course the responsibility rested, came to the decision to make into a permanent part of the parochial life what had been a very valuable and distinctive feature of the mission. He knew already, or, if he did not, many reminded him, that the lack of community-sense in the village made every new venture, however brilliantly inaugurated, likely to collapse after a few weeks or months; some of his people were suspicious of the service as seeming too much like a "stunt"; others objected to the crudity of the music or said that they "liked a quiet service." All these difficulties were carefully and prayerfully weighed, and set against the principles of the thing. Reflection made it luminously clear that a village, even one so loosely-knit as this, was a God-given " field " [1] for the growth of the " Church family-sense "; and that the secret of the development of that "family-sense" lay in making the Eucharist the centre of both worship and fellowship.

The incumbent was driven, too, to see that indi-

---

[1] For instance, the parish priest in a village is still generally accepted as a natural leader of the community; he alone has the " right of entry " (usually with a welcome) into every house in " his " parish.

vidualistic objections, based on what people "like" or "don't like," could have no final weight against what was plainly the right principle. What was needed to counteract these was an education in the whole conception of corporate Christianity. Some of the objections came from non-parishioners, but it had now become abundantly clear that the parish church existed primarily and essentially for the parishioners, and that others, however devout and however interested, must not determine the policy of the parish. It was hard to part with the children's Eucharist, until it was realised that the right plan, and the one with the greatest promise for the future, was to work for the parents to come themselves to the Parish Eucharist, and bring their children with them.[1] One suggestion, of a more constructive type than most, called for special consideration: "Why not have the Parish Communion monthly?" The experience of other priests was sought here, and the unanimous answer came that this would "stereotype" the habit of monthly communion, whereas an essential part of the new system was the encouragement, in every possible way, of Communion *every* Sunday, the weekly gathering of the family in the Father's house, round the Father's table.[2]

So the adventure was made, although for the time at least it was necessary to abandon the idea of making

[1] The prevailing practice on the part of parents of sending their children but not attending themselves is likely to " inoculate " children against churchgoing later on. They are having instilled into them week by week that attendance at public worship is something for children, which is discarded on reaching maturity.

[2] For further discussion of this point see De Candole, *The Sacraments and the Church*, pp. 143–6 (Mowbray, 1935).

the Parish Eucharist the *one communion* on the Lord's Day, the centre and symbol of the unity of Christ's people in the village, and the compromise was adopted of continuing the 8 a.m. celebration for those communicants who would not accept the Parish Communion.[1]   But, in spite of this, in eighteen months the new system had become pretty firmly established. What is more, its effects on character were beginning to show themselves in real changes of life, in growing loyalty to our Lord and readiness to serve Him in His Church; as well as in a marked growth of the right kind of community-spirit in the village. Among other things which, directly or indirectly, were connected with the Parish Eucharist or its progenitor, the parochial mission, may be mentioned the following: (*a*) the provision, in spite of financial stringency, of a lady worker; (*b*) a church housing scheme to meet the urgent need for better accommodation for villagers on the lowest wage-level (the first batch of cottages is about to be constructed); (*c*) a Church Mission of Fellowship to the Londoners who come to the parish each autumn for hop-picking. So God richly blessed the venture, granting ever-fresh visions of " things that He would have done," for faith and courage to grasp.

A few words must suffice about practical details. The service is simply sung to Martin Shaw's " Anglican

[1] These consisted, in the main, of people who would call themselves " instructed Catholics," the majority of those who gladly accepted the Parish Communion being people of " Evangelical " sympathies.   Potentially the Parish Communion is a very significant meeting-point for " Catholics " who wish to come to their communion fasting, and " Evangelicals " who have scruples about " non-communicating attendance."   But party-spirit causes so much hardening of heart that it is likely to be a rather slow business in practice.

Folk-Mass " or Royle Shore's " Merbecke." There is a small choir, but the congregation is learning to take its full part. Ceremonial is simplified and made as " sincere " and intelligible as possible. Plain cards with the chief parts of the service and simple directions for following have been printed at a trifling cost and are available for the congregation. There is a short " liturgical " sermon, almost always based on the Epistle or Gospel or both, and usually directed at showing the practical application of the " message " of the Sunday to practical everyday life, the life of the Christian " in the world," but not " of " it.

The preparation of the breakfast gives no great trouble. A rota of fourteen members of the congregation was formed, two at a time preparing sandwiches (potted meat on ordinary days, ham on high days) and laying tables overnight. The kettles are put on to boil in the vicarage during the service. Sandwiches and bread-and-marmalade, with tea, provide a *menu* well appreciated. There is no definite charge, but people are asked to put what they can in a bowl at the end; adults usually give fourpence, and children two-pence or threepence. This system has not only paid its way, but has accumulated balance enough to buy crockery, cutlery and other accessories for the breakfast. The breakfast itself has always proved a most cheerful meal, and incidentally gives the parish priest a weekly opportunity of an informal talk with some of his keenest people about plans for the parish.

The system outlined above brings a most satisfying assurance to a parish priest (and probably to the laity too), that here is something which really " makes sense " of Christianity, and this itself is a powerful

K

factor making for " unity of spirit "; but the priest who
intends to adopt it must be prepared also for great
disappointment.   He will, for instance, probably find
that many or most of those who have grown up with
individualist ideas of the Sacrament, whether their
outlook is Catholic or Evangelical, will oppose the
change, perhaps most resolutely.   These may include
some of his best workers and most faithful layfolk.
This may easily be the biggest of all the burdens that
the priest has to bear, but he will be comforted with
the knowledge that our Blessed Lord had the same
kind of misunderstanding, often from His chosen dis-
ciples.   No faithful priest can merely " agree to
differ "; he must pray and work patiently for these
sheep to come into the fold.   " Love will find a way,"
though it may be years before results are visible, and
in some cases it may be that a real conversion is what
is needed.

It is more than likely also that dissensions will occur
from time to time within the " family " itself, perhaps all
the more because people who would not ordinarily meet
much are thrown very closely together.   It is encouraging to find that this very tendency soon made itself manifest in the earliest days, and gave occasion to St. Paul's
great teaching about the body and its members, with
their several functions, who must learn to act together
in harmony.[1]   In fact, one most important part of

---

[1] The clearest N.T. passage is in 1 Cor. 12, but cf. also Rom. 12.
3–17; 14. 3 ff; 15. 1, 2; 16. 17, 1 Cor. 1. 10 ff., 1 Cor. 11 *passim*,
Phil. 4. 2, etc.   The Parish Communion and the " family-sense "
which grows up round it will make the Epistles of St. Paul " come
alive " to the understanding reader.   Most parishes can easily
recognise Syntyche and Euodia; cf. also *The Parish Communion*
(S.P.C.K.), especially pp. 92–94.

Christian fellowship is this difficult business of helping people of very different temperaments to find unity with each other. Yet it is what God does again and again through the Parish Communion, where men and women are ready in humble faith to seek His guidance. It is therefore no wonder that " the Devil hates Christian fellowship." It is worth noticing, too, that the closer the family life, the more readily will the parish priest be able to detect and to cope with these dissensions as they occur. How necessary that he should be a man of constant prayer and reliance on the Holy Spirit!

One thing remains to be mentioned. It will naturally be found that this " Church family-sense " and the desire for greater unity within the parish, as they grow, will make for a better understanding not only of the Eucharist, but also of the other great " sacrament of the Gospel." It will become plain that Holy Baptism, which has so tremendous a place in the New Testament, has been largely neglected and misunderstood. (1) Part of the process of recovery will surely be the restoration of Baptism as invariably a solemn public ceremony; (2) as the pressure of paganism increases, more and more will Baptism be a ceremony for adults, marking a deliberate renunciation of the world of darkness, and entry, after due instruction, into the Kingdom of light, " before the face of the congregation "; (3) infant Baptism will only be permitted in those cases where both parents (and sponsors) are practising members of the Christian community (" right inside the family ") and are willing to undergo, when necessary, a careful and systematic course of instruction in the principles of sponsorship.

II

THE LITURGY AND THE SCRIPTURES

By A. G. HEBERT, S.S.M.

THE various essays in this book describe the Parish Communion movement, as it finds expression to-day in various places in town and country, at home and overseas. The object of this essay is to affirm that the fruitfulness of this movement will depend, more than anything else, on the extent to which it is rooted and grounded in the Scriptures. The liturgy is the expression in worship of that mystery of grace by which the Church lives. Holy Scripture is a canon, or standard, of the Church's life, as being for all time the classical and normative expression of that same mystery of grace. The Sacrament is a "visible word," setting forth those same spiritual realities which the written word of God sets forth. Therefore the Scriptures, having at the first been written in and for the Church of the Old Covenant and of the New, are not intelligible apart from the life and worship of the Church; and conversely, the meaning of the life and worship of the Church is explained in the Scriptures, of which, directly or indirectly, almost the whole of the Church's liturgy is made up.

The parish priests who contribute these descriptions of

the Parish Communion will not have said much about their own sermons. These must of necessity be short, not more than five or ten minutes; and I expect they consist usually of admirable expositions of the Scriptures for the day in relation to the common act of worship and communion. For the Parish Communion of itself provides exactly that setting in which the Scriptures become intelligible and luminous, since here the people are met together in that Assembly of the Church of which St. Paul is thinking when he writes to " the Church of God which is at Corinth "; they are met as the People of God, as the New Israel, to worship God. That is the precise setting in and for which the Scriptures were written. The Gospels, as modern study has shown, were not written merely as memoirs or chronicles of our Lord's life; the various stories told of Him took shape as stories told in the Church and to the Church about Jesus the Messiah, the Saviour, the ascended Lord, the Head of the Body. The Epistles were written to the various communities to tell the Christians there assembled *what they are*, what their Christian calling is, what their life in the Church means. The same applies to the Old Testament, the Book of the Old Israel; thus the Psalms, as collected in the Psalter for use in temple and synagogue, express the liturgical prayer and praise of the People of God under the Old Covenant, and as such were taken over and used by the Israel of the New Covenant. Hence the primary duty of the Christian preacher is to expound the Scriptures, not merely devotionally, in relation to the religious life of the individual, but theologically, to explain what the status of the Christians in relation to God actually is.

All Christian theology is there, in the Scriptures, not as regards all the forms and expressions of it, but as regards the meat and substance of it. It is there, not, for the most part, in an abstract, formulated form, but in a simple, concrete form. The layman, we are told, is impatient of theology. In so far as this is so, is it not because we have given him the impression that theology consists of abstract doctrines, deeply interesting to the theologian engaged in worrying them out and getting them clear, but not to the ordinary person whose concern is with the practical things of life? Have we not wearied our people by presenting theology to the layman in the form suited to the specialist?

Yet the layman needs theology, because he needs a belief, in the light of which to live his daily life in the world; and alike in the Bible and in the liturgy, theology is expressed not abstractly but concretely, by means of symbols and images; and it is through the liturgy, through the things which the layman sees and hears and does in church, that he chiefly imbibes his theology. " From the point of view of the historian it cannot be too vigorously insisted on that it is liturgy and devotion which are the really formative element in the religion and ' culture ' (in the sense of the whole system of accepted ethics and unquestioned assumptions and instinctive mental attitudes) of the immense dumb but praying multitudes which form the strength of Christianity in every age." [1]

Bible and liturgy alike teach us theology by means of likenesses drawn from visible and earthly things. One such series of images is drawn from natural birth. The first thing in the process of birth is the love of the

[1] Gregory Dix, *The Apostolic Tradition of St. Hippolytus*, p. xliii.

man for the woman; and this is explicitly taken by
St. Paul in Ephes. 5. 25–32 as the likeness of the love
of Christ for the Church, which indeed throughout the
New Testament is called His Bride; a variant of the
same appears in our Lord's own parables of the Great
Supper and the Ten Virgins. After marriage comes
birth. Of the Church, our Mother, we are born again
through Baptism and made children of God, born
again " not of blood, nor of the will of the flesh, nor
of the will of man, but of God." The new life that we
have in Christ is just as much *given*, not earned by any
activity of ours, as is the natural life that we received
of our parents. As children we call upon " Our
Father, which art in heaven " (crying Abba, Father);
as His children, we are thereby made brothers and
sisters of all the other children in His universal spiritual
Family. In the spiritual as in the natural family there
is nurture and upbringing, the family hearth, the family
table, the common meal. When we sin, we are like
the Prodigal Son, in that we have strayed away from
our home, and the door of that home stands open against
our return.

Baptism uses this image. Christian Baptism, like
the Jewish baptism used for the admission of proselytes,
is a rite of initiation; and St. Paul sees in the dis-
appearance of the candidate under the water and his
emergence from it a likeness of the burial of Christ in
the tomb and His rising again, and a likeness of the
burying of this person's old life and his new birth to
the new life in Christ (*see* Rom. 6. 3–11). With the
likenesses that we have mentioned, drawn from birth
and the family, Baptism combines others; above all
the act of washing from the filth of the old sinful

nature. The traditional ceremonial of Baptism combines other likenesses also, such as the anointing, with its connections with ancient sacrificial ritual, and with the word " Christ "; the clothing in a white robe; and the giving of a lighted taper.

All these likenesses are drawn from common, everyday things; that is true of the rites and ceremonies of the Church in general, and it is true of the Scriptures which the Church has in her hand as she performs her sacred rites. It is not too much to say that all the teaching of the Scriptures about God's redemptive work for us and the meaning of our redeemed life is built up of likenesses drawn from visible and everyday things. " I am the living *Bread* which came down from heaven." " Ho, every one that *thirsteth*, come ye to the waters." " *Put ye on* the Lord Jesus Christ." " *Cast off* the works of darkness." " I am the Light of the world." The Kingdom of Heaven is compared to a field of wheat, because souls grow much in the same way as plants, and to a feast, and to a landlord employing servants, and to a man seeking pearls, and to a net cast into the sea, and to leaven, and to many other things, sometimes in detailed parables, but also in the words used to describe the things of the spirit. Sin is *hamartia* (wrong aim, wrong direction), transgression (going off the right path), lawlessness (breaking laws); it is described as a state of perishing, a state of being lost, a " walking in the darkness," a blindness, an enmity with God and with man, a filthiness, a state of being diseased.

Out of these images and likenesses the cloth of the Scriptures is woven; always the heavenly and spiritual is interpreted by means of the earthly and natural.

There will be no sense on the part of the layman that theology is dull, when it is interpreted to him by the preacher in the way that Scripture itself uses, and that the liturgy uses too. " Open Thou mine eyes, that I may see the wondrous things of Thy law."

At the Holy Eucharist the Epistle is read to us. It is ordinarily the message of an Apostle, St. Peter, St. John, or St. Paul standing up *in medio Ecclesiæ* (see English Hymnal, No. 665), to speak to the Christians the word that has been given him to say. He tells the Christians what they are: " strangers and pilgrims," on their way through this world to the heavenly City to which they belong, the Jerusalem which is above, and is free. Therefore they must beware of the dangers which beset them on the road, and " abstain from fleshly lusts." Or the Apostle addresses the assembled Church directly, in words which express the right relation of a Christian Minister to his people: " I thank my God upon every remembrance of you . . . for your fellowship in the Gospel from the first day until now, being confident of this very thing, that He who hath begun a good work in you will perform it until the day of Jesus Christ; even as it is meet for me to think thus of you all, because I have you in my heart." This may sound remote when it is thought of as a bit of evidence for the student of religion, throwing light on the religion of the Apostolic Age; but it comes very near indeed to-day when it is read in an assembly of Christians who have a clear sense of their community and fellowship with one another as a Christian congregation.

Private devotional reading of the Bible is a good thing; for every soul is alone with God, and every

Christian is a pilgrim on the way to the City. But it is only when the Scriptures are read in the light of our common life in the Church that we can enter properly into their meaning. The Bible is the Book of the People of God. From the Bible we learn what the life of the Church really means; and it is only in the context of our life in the Church that we rightly understand the Bible. This is as true of the liturgical Gospel as it is of the Epistle.

We treat the Gospel with great ceremonial reverence, and we stand to listen to it, because in the Gospel we have the words and acts of the Lord Himself, the same Lord who in His Sacrament is Priest and Victim, and Host at the Lord's Supper.

Many of the liturgical Gospels consist of accounts of miracles of healing. These are not read as mere incidents from the Gospel history; for it would not be of great interest to us merely to hear how one paralysed man among a million was fortunate enough to be healed, or how one widow had her dead son restored to life, only to escape for a few years the death that must in any case overtake him a little later. The Gospel lections only become intelligible when we see them not as mere isolated incidents, but as pictures of the universal activity of the Saviour of mankind, the Christ of the Gospel and of the Sacrament, who deals with us and with all the members of His universal Family as He dealt with those people then.

Thus, on Quinquagesima Sunday we hear first our Lord prophesying His Passion and Resurrection, and then see Him heal blind Bartimæus. The meaning is that I am Bartimæus. I hear the Lord and His saints pass by, going on the Way of the Cross, and I ask what

it means; for I do not understand the mystery of the
Cross, nor do I see that the suffering which is going on
around me has a redemptive meaning. But I cry to
Him for light; I pray, " Lord, that I may receive my
sight." When He has opened my eyes that I may see,
then I shall follow Him and His saints in the Way,
through Lent and Passiontide to the glory of the
Resurrection.

Thus the Gospels illuminate for us our approach to
the altar; they show us Christ in relation to His
Church. They give us words in which we may speak
to our Lord:

> " The dogs eat of the crumbs which fall from their
> masters' table. Lord, help me."
> " Lord, I am not worthy that Thou shouldest
> come under my roof."

And words which we are to hear Him speak:

> " Son, be of good cheer; thy sins be forgiven
> thee."
> " O woman, great is thy faith; be it unto thee
> even as thou wilt."
> " Ye have not chosen Me, but I have chosen
> you, and ordained you, that ye should go and
> bring forth fruit, and that your fruit should
> remain."

Thus in the Gospels, as in the Epistles, we see the
mystery of the Church set forth. It is no accident that
a story of a Feeding of the Multitude is read for the
Gospel on no less than three Sundays out of fifty-two;
for we have there a likeness of the Eucharist. It is no

doubt for the same reason that this subject comes six
times in the four Gospels.

> " Reveal Him, we entreat Thee, to our faith.
>   Show Him unto us coming forth with gifts from His Sacrifice :
>   A Shepherd, feeding His flock :
>   A Master, comforting His servants ;
>   A King, feasting with His people."[1]

Likewise the Psalms are used in the Church service
as the prayer of the Church, speaking to God through
Jesus Christ. The Psalter, as we have seen, was the
liturgical book of Old Israel; the Church took it over
and saw its meaning made complete in Christ. Thus
Ps. 22, the psalm of the suffering Servant of the Lord,
becomes the psalm of Christ's passion; the royal Ps. 72
becomes a psalm of Christ's universal kingship.

In other words, in the Psalter we hear the voice of
mankind speaking to God; for Christ is the Head of
the human race, and the Church is nothing else than
humanity redeemed to God through Christ. Thus the
Psalms are much more than individual religious
poems; the religious experience which they col-
lectively contain is much wider than that of any
individual Christian. They express not *my* prayer and

---

[1] From the Presbyterian *Book of Common Order*, 1928 (Oxford
University Press), p. 65.

A simple exposition of the Collects, Epistles, and Gospels for
all the days in the Prayer Book, on the lines here described, by
the Rev. A. G. Hebert and the Rev. D. N. Allenby, has been
published by S.P.C.K. at 1s. 6d.; also in six pamphlets at 2d.
each; with the title *Pray with the Church*. An older book, *Praeparatio*,
in two volumes, for Sundays and Holy-days respectively, with a
preface by Fr. Congreve, S.S.J.E., can probably be still bought
second-hand. Another book that is to be highly recommended is
By Faith with Thanksgiving, by the Rt. Rev. Philip Loyd, Bishop of
Nasik (Mowbray, 1s. 6d.) ; this consists of a devotional exercise
for each Sunday, drawn from the materials provided by the service
for the day.

praise, but *our* prayer and praise; or, rather, Christ's, and ours only as we move away from our isolated self-hood and speak as members of Him and members of one another. They are something common, in which we join; we recite them in the name of all, and with all, and for all. We watch others reciting them, we watch the Church reciting them; with them, and in her, we too join in.

The singing of the Psalms formed in the ancient Church a very prominent feature of the eucharistic liturgy; the relics of this remain in the Introits, Graduals, etc., of the Latin rite. It was a very serious loss to the Church of England when in the 1552 Prayer Book all this psalmody disappeared. It is a matter for consideration whether a psalm may not well be sung as the Introit or Gradual at the Parish Communion in place of the customary hymn.[1]

We should also notice that the Liturgical Movement in the Roman Catholic Church is to a large extent a movement back to the Scriptures; for in restoring to the people their active part in the service and putting back the Missal into their hands, it is teaching them to pray in the words of the Bible; the variable part of the rite, consisting of the Introit, etc., the three Collects, and the lections, is for the most part taken from the Bible, and forms a collection of Scriptural material selected and arranged for liturgical use. We hear of wonderful results following, when, under the guidance of the Belgian Benedictines, the faithful learn to meditate together on the Scriptural texts in the Missal. We in the Church of England can say that the Bible has been in the hands of the people, and that we have

[1] See my book *Liturgy and Society*, pp. 72–5, 214–20.

had a vernacular liturgy, for nearly 400 years; we have less right to say that we know how to use these things.

There is, however, one further point that must be raised. We have been outlining an exposition of the Scriptures largely on the lines of the traditional mystical interpretation. Does this involve turning our backs on the methods and results of modern critical study? The answer must be an emphatic No. The careful and accurate study of the " literal sense " and the original meaning of the Scriptures is indispensable to save the exposition from becoming not only ignorant, but also fanciful and trivial. Indeed, we ought to claim that the best exposition of the kind we have been describing would be that which was most truly on the lines of the original meaning. It is not arbitrary to find the Passion of Christ in the Psalms; for there is a continuity of principle between the sufferings of the Old Testament saints and those of Israel's Messiah; and it is this that is chiefly meant when our Lord and the Apostles say that His Passion is " according to the Scriptures." Thus the exposition of the liturgical Gospel that we have described would appear to reproduce very closely the narration of the Gospel stories in the Apostolic Church as Form-criticism sees it.

It is indeed true that many scholars in modern times have been accustomed to interpret the Scriptures on the basis not of the theology of the Bible itself, but of the humanistic and evolutionary ideas which have dominated our culture since the " Enlightenment " of the eighteenth century; they have looked on the Old Testament, not as the book of the Covenant of God with Israel, but as the record of the development of Hebrew religious ideas from the crudities of the Book of Judges to the noble monotheism of the Second Isaiah, and on the New Testament as the record of the progressive deification of Him who was the supreme Teacher and Example. But that is to interpret the Bible in the light of a theology which is fundamentally alien to the Bible; and the Christian teacher does not get much help here. There is, however, another side to the matter. Science is a gift of God: the careful and exact study of history is a gift of God. The Liberal scholars have carried out a vast amount of excellent investigation, and results of permanent value have been reached. But the best modern scholars— such as, in the New Testament field, Hoskyns, Dodd, Vincent Taylor, Manson—while fully accepting the methods of critical investigation, give us an interpretation of a quite different character, far more sympathetic to the ideas of the Biblical writers themselves.

In truth there is no conflict to-day between the Church's view of the Bible and the interpretation of it given by the best scholarship. But the two lie on different levels. Critical study deals with historical facts and the evidence for them, on the level of natural knowledge. Theological exposition deals with the word of divine truth, on the level of Revelation. The conclusion is, not that critical study is irrelevant to the preacher's message, but that it is essential to it; *gratia non tollit naturam, sed perficit.* The very fact that the Christian Gospel claims to be a Revelation that has taken place in history, necessitates an appeal to history which must be vindicated by historical investigation. The Church gives us the New Testament as the testimony of the Apostles to the historical facts; therefore the New Testament must be examined by all the historical tests that are available. She gives us the New Testament also as containing the message of that Revelation, whose spiritual reality the preacher is set to expound. Therefore the exposition of spiritual truth on the higher level must not ignore but presuppose the critical study of the historical facts on the lower level.

But it is clear that historical investigation is the work of the specialist; and also that, in so far as the ordinary layman needs to study these things, the place for this is not the pulpit, but a tutorial class, where there is opportunity for reading and for questions and discussion. But the Word of God, the message of spiritual truth, is for all, learned and unlearned alike. The study of this is indeed just as much an intellectual study as the other; it calls for the fullest exercise of thought and understanding. But, as we have said, it lies on a different level; and the sermon needs to be followed, not by discussion and criticism, but by quiet recollection and appropriation.

The primary duty of the preacher is to expound the Scriptures. At the Parish Communion there is time to do something in this way, but not much; and it is necessary to find some other time for this. There is Sunday evening; and here the question is worth asking why it is usually considered necessary to keep the sermon till the end of the service, when the people are already tired, having been occupied in religious exercises for forty or forty-five minutes. Is it not in every way better to put the sermon after the Third Collect, or even after the Second Lesson, in the place where the Prayer Book expects the children to be catechised? There is also the latter part of Sunday morning; for if the Parish Communion and breakfast are over by 11 o'clock or soon after, two hours remain of which use can be made. In many places this can be profitably used for the instruction of the younger children, and for tutorial classes for young people. But it is also possible that in some places on some Sundays in the year a service might be held at 11.30 or 12 which would consist mainly of a sermon lasting some forty-five minutes, in which there would be opportunity to treat a subject with some thoroughness. As the spirit of common worship which the Parish Communion generates gives the key to the right understanding of the Scriptures, so it should be the case that its influence should be felt in all else that is done, and the spoken word of the preacher reflect the visible word of the Sacrament, and set forth a Scriptural theology in terms that the people can understand.

Moreover, this Scriptural theology consists not in the first place of ideals to be aimed at, but of realities and facts: the facts of what God is, what He has made His world to be, and who Christ is, and what Christ has made us to be, and what we are through the Holy Spirit dwelling in us. The following words of the Rev. V. A. Demant might well be framed and hung up in every priest's study:

" Tell people only what they must do, and you will numb them into despair; you will turn the Gospel into a shabby replica of the world's irreligious and nagging moralism, with its oceanfulls of good advice. But tell them what they are, of their dignity as made in the image of

L

God, and that their sins are wicked perversions of their nature . . . tell them that the world with its horrors is still God's world, though its true order is upside down; tell them that they can do all things through Christ, because in Him all the powers of their nature are directed and brought to fruition . . . and you will help to revive hope in this dispirited generation." [1]

[1] *Christian Polity*, Faber and Faber, 1936, p. 39.

APPENDIX 1

THE EUCHARIST IN EARLY DAYS

The Primitive Church at Jerusalem

(*a*) THEN they that gladly received his word were baptised: and the same day there were added unto them about three thousand souls. And they continued steadfastly in the apostles' doctrine and fellowship, and in breaking of bread, and in prayers.

And all that believed were together, and had all things common; and sold their possessions and goods, and parted them to all men, as every man had need. And they, continuing daily with one accord in the temple, and breaking bread from house to house, did eat their meat with gladness and singleness of heart, praising God, and having favour with all the people.

(Acts 2. 41–2, 44–7.)

(*b*) And on the Lord's day of the Lord come together and break bread and give thanks, having first confessed your transgressions, that our sacrifice may be pure. But whoso hath a dispute with his fellow, let him not come together with you, until they be reconciled, that our sacrifice be not polluted. For this is that which was spoken of by the Lord: In every place and time offer me a pure sacrifice; for I am a great

King, saith the Lord, and my name is wonderful among the Gentiles. . . .

. . . As this bread that was broken is scattered upon the mountains, and gathered together, and became one, so let thy Church be gathered together from the ends of the earth into thy kingdom: for thine is the glory and the power through Jesus Christ for ever.

> (From *The Teaching of the Twelve Apostles*, a very early Christian writing, possibly about A.D. 100, perhaps from the mountains of Syria.)

(*c*) It is their habit on a fixed day to assemble before daylight and sing by turns a hymn to Christ as God; and to bind themselves by an oath (*or* "sacrament"), not for any crime, but not to commit theft or robbery or adultery and not to break their word. . . . After this, they depart, and meet together again to take food, but ordinary and harmless food.

> (From the letter of Pliny, the pagan Governor of Bithynia, on the southern coast of the Black Sea, about A.D. 110, written to ask the Roman Emperor how he is to treat these Christians whom he does not understand.)

(*d*) On the so-called day of the Sun all who live in cities or in the country gather together to one place, and the memoirs of the Apostles (*the Gospels*) or the writings of the prophets (*Lessons from the Old Testament, or of Christian writers, corresponding to the Epistle*) are read, as long as time allows. Then when the reader has ceased, the president (*or celebrant*) gives by word of mouth his admonition and exhortation to follow these good things (*Sermon on the Sunday Scriptures*). Then we all rise together and offer prayers; and when we have ceased to pray, bread is brought and wine and water (*the Offertory*), and the president in like manner offers up prayers and thanksgivings (*the Eucharistic Prayer or Prayer of Consecration*) according to his ability, and the people assent saying Amen (*Amen after the Consecration*). Then follows the distribution to each and the partaking of that for which thanks were given (*the Communion*); and to them that are absent a portion is sent by the deacons.

. . . And this food is called among us Eucharist, of which it is not lawful for any man to partake but he who believes our teaching to be true, and has been washed with the washing which is for the remission of sins and for regeneration, and is so living as Christ commanded. For not as common bread and common drink do we receive these; but as Jesus Christ our Saviour being made flesh through the Word of God took both flesh and blood for our salvation, so also were we taught that the food for which thanks (or Eucharist) are given by the word of prayer that comes from Him . . . is both flesh and blood of that Jesus who was made flesh. . . .

. . . Of those that are well-to-do and willing, every one gives what he will according to his own purpose, and the collection is deposited with the president, and he it is that succours orphans and widows, and those that are in want through sickness or any other cause. . . .

(From the *Apology* of Justin Martyr, an explanation of Christianity for the Roman Emperor, written at Rome about A.D. 150).

APPENDIX 2

A DESCRIPTION AND PLAN OF JOHN KEBLE CHURCH, MILL HILL

By D. F. MARTIN-SMITH

THE planning of the Church is the result of an attempt to satisfy the requirements of certain aims and needs of the parish, amongst which the family Communion and breakfast which follows stand out in importance.

The Church Hall was therefore linked to the church, the " link " taking the form of a colonnade which leads to the centre of the building.

Internally it was required that there should be an impression of unity, and arranged in fact so that the unit—that is to say, the congregation—could be grouped closely round the sanctuary, and the church takes the form of a square nave and two aisles with no dividing supports, forming a clear space some 70 feet by 50 feet, with a very wide and comparatively shallow sanctuary, which is thus almost part of the nave.

The choir has been considered as a portion of the congregation having a musical responsibility, and as such is divided from the rest of the seating by low walls or " cancelli."

Priests' return stalls are at the west end of this enclosure, as is also the organ console.

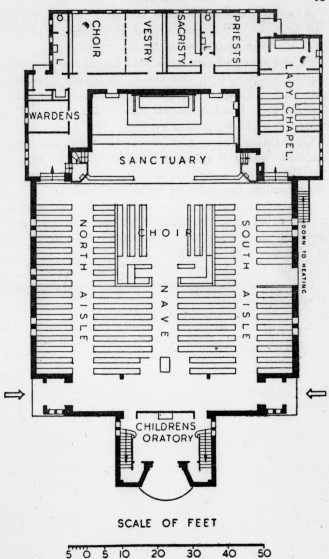

SCALE OF FEET

5 0 5 10   20   30   40   50

A space has been formed amongst the seating at the west end of the church in which the font is placed, so that it is in clear view of the congregation.

At the west end also, separated by pillars, is a clear entrance space, with porches at each end, and fully provided with spaces for notices, literature, collecting boxes, etc. Leading from this space, through a screen, is a children's oratory.

Over this is formed a gallery, in the north and south ends of which is the organ itself, with the central portion left free for extra seats, either for overflow of congregation, for orchestra, or for additional choir.

A Lady Chapel is approached through an opening at the east end of the south aisle, and is treated as a separate unit, and forms a contrast with the large clear space of the combined aisles and nave.

Behind the sanctuary is a corridor approached from either side which gives access to various vestries and cloakrooms.

The plan is reproduced by courtesy of the Royal Institute of British Architects.

APPENDIX 3

A LETTER TO A CONGREGATION

after the change from the Sung Eucharist at 11 to the Parish Communion at 9.15 had been decided upon: written by an outside priest.

IT is a great venture of faith when the priest and people of a parish decide to alter the time of the chief Sunday service. It means giving up an order of things to which they have been accustomed, and taking a step in the dark, not knowing how it will turn out. For it is impossible in the nature of things that the people should have had experience of the benefits and blessings which they are told the change will bring till they have tried it, and indeed, till they have tried it for some considerable time. So, while I would congratulate with all my heart a parish which proposes to make this change, I think the people of the parish need some encouragement in making this venture of faith; and so far as lies in my power, I would wish to give them this encouragement. For I think you must feel rather like a bather venturing into the water for the first time, who knows that he will enjoy it very much after he gets in and will feel refreshed and comfortable afterwards, but who shrinks from the first plunge.

It would not be difficult to write a treatise to show that the Holy Eucharist in the Christian Church is always by rights a communion service. In the early Church the Eucharist on the Lord's Day was always the general communion. So it is, in theory, in the Orthodox Churches, where the " low celebration " is unknown. So it is according to the intention of the Prayer Book, which clearly envisages the communion of the people throughout the service. So it is according to the text even of the Roman Missal, where the Canon of the Mass presupposes a general communion, as do most of the old post-communion collects.

But how did the sung Eucharist without communion of the people arise? Simply because during the early Middle Ages the people stopped coming to communion; the communicants gradually dwindled till at last there were none. In the Middle Ages as a rule people received communion once a year. This was one of the things which the Reformation tried to correct and which the Roman Church has since set to work to correct.

But how did we in the Church of England get into the habit of the sung Eucharist without communion of the people? It happened in the course of the Catholic Revival, from about 1860 onwards. We ought not to criticise the men who did it; many of them were saints, men like Lowder, Maconochie and Stanton. It was fixed in the popular mind that the hour of the chief service on Sunday must be 11 a.m. The Holy Eucharist must be the chief service. And communion must be received fasting. That was how they got to it; there was also the example of the English mediæval Church and the modern Roman

Church. Perhaps at that time it was not possible for anything else to be done.

But now, it is no exaggeration to say that the mind of the Church is coming to see that the way of the Parish Communion is the right way. Here are two indications. A book of essays has lately appeared, entitled *The Parish Communion*, of which nearly 2000 copies were sold in less than a year. I have been on these last two Sundays preaching at four London churches, where the 11 a.m. sung Mass is established. Each of the four vicars, as soon as I mentioned that on the previous Sunday I had been to a Parish Communion at 9.30 followed by a parish breakfast, spontaneously remarked that of course this was the right thing: in one case the vicar and two curates exclaimed in chorus, " Oh, how good! That is what it ought to be." None of the four churches are ready as yet to take the plunge; but you know (or would know if you were able to talk to many clergy) that every parish priest regards his own parish as a peculiarly difficult one; and I believe that the time is approaching when there will be something like a general move. At any rate it is clear that very many clergy are thinking hard about it.

There are, I fully admit, some parishes which cannot and ought not to make this change for the present; as for instance, some central city churches, where the actual area of the parish is almost uninhabited at night, as it consists almost entirely of offices, warehouses, and shops; and perhaps some country parishes, where the farmers have a great deal of work to do on Sunday mornings. But these present a problem which is not easily answered; some country parishes—I could name five or six—are very happy with a Parish Communion at or about 9 a.m.; other clergy say they can't get their people before 11. Also there are "residential" parishes, where all the houses have servants, and the servants prepare breakfast for the family at 9 and dinner at 1, so that the " family " go—or don't go—to church at 11; and these certainly present a special problem.

But for the ordinary working-class parish, where the people live in the parish, and there are few or no houses with servants, 9 or 9.30 seems to offer every advantage. Time to get back and cook the Sunday dinner after Mass. A longer rest on the Lord's Day, the day of rest, for those who have to be up very early during the week. An opportunity for a meeting of the congregation at a breakfast in the Parish Hall—by all experience, a blessed and happy institution. For the priest, a chance to use the later part of Sunday morning for classes, children's instruction, and so on; and for the young people, sometimes at least, a chance to go out into the country and be back in time for Evensong. But above all, the service itself: above all, that the Holy Eucharist becomes not a ceremonial performed in the sanctuary at which we look on, but a sacred action in which we take our full part, exercising the priesthood of the laity and being ourselves, through our communion, offered up in sacrifice, as members of Christ's mystical Body. Holy Communion comes to be, not an occasional, monthly, or quarterly act of devotion, but the regular food of our Christian life, the meeting-point of the mystical Body of Christ which is His Church.

APPENDIX 4

THE PARISH COMMUNION [1]

Some Suggestions and Hints for Communicants

The Eucharist is the action, not of a number of private persons, but of the Church as a whole. We come not to " take Communion " for ourselves, but to make " our Communion "—as a body; that is, to make an act of common offering. It is a family occasion, when all should take their full share in the worship, as communicants, for without Communion the action is incomplete. The act of Communion is the common meal of the Christian family with each other and their unseen but present Lord. Those who " have duly received these holy Mysteries . . . are very members incorporate in the mystical Body of Christ, which is the blessed company of all faithful people." The action is shared by as many worshippers as possible; in addition to the priest, who as leader expresses in word and action that for which the whole congregation has come together, there are the clerk, taperers, thurifer and crucifer; choir and organ to lead the singing and wardens to bring the offerings of the people. The normal service is that at which

[1] This paper is largely condensed from the *Church's Offering*, by H. de Caudole (Mowbray, 1s. 6d.)

the largest possible number assist. ALL have their share and ALL should join in the Responses, Creed, Confession, Lord's Prayer, Gloria, and *not least in the great Scriptural Amen to the Eucharistic act of Consecration*, which sets the seal of the whole congregation on the priest's words and acts.

The Preparation

The priest and his attendants enter, kneel at the foot of the altar, and say a short private preparation. Meanwhile all sing the INTROIT PSALM or Hymn, and the priest ascends to the altar and censes it. Incense has been used in Christian worship from the first, and is the most ancient, most universal and most significant symbol of prayer, burnt as it is offered and giving out in its burning a sweet savour. The priest begins the service with the great family prayer, the OUR FATHER and a COLLECT FOR PURITY; these two prayers originally formed part of the priest's private preparation, and are therefore said by him alone. Then the Church turns to the cry for mercy, the KYRIE ELEISON nine times repeated, "*Lord, have mercy.*" All worship must begin with penitence.

The Ministry of the Word

The Collect, Epistle and Gospel, varying week by week, follow next, setting the note for the particular season or day. The regular succession of season to season in the round of the Church's year brings before us the different phases of God's great self-revelation, from Advent through Christmas and Epiphany to Lent, Passiontide and Easter, the Great Forty Days, Ascensiontide, Pentecost and Trinity. Year by year the instructed Christian grows deeper and deeper in the understanding of the mysteries of the Faith.

The COLLECT gathers up in brief, concentrated form the special thought of God suggested by the day or season and the petition based upon it. The Lesson or EPISTLE (normally from one of the Epistles of the New Testament) is concerned with practical Christian life. While the Epistle is read all should sit.

After the Epistle all join in singing the GRADUAL PSALM or Hymn (so called because it was sung on the steps (*gradus*) of the Altar), while the Gospel Procession is forming up.

The GOSPEL contains the words and actions of Christ Himself. The congregation rise and stand to listen to His words; the Procession comes forth from the sanctuary, a telling picture of the Church going out to carry the message to the world—the Cross at her head, the tapers symbolising the light she bears, the incense the " sweet savour " of Christ, all moving out into the body of the church and there facing north, where the sun never shines, to proclaim the coming of the glorious light of the knowledge of God in the face of Jesus Christ. The announcement of the Gospel is welcomed by the Response " *Glory be to Thee, O Lord,*" and its close by " *Praise be to Thee, O Christ,*" which should be sung by all.

All is summed up in the CREED, the triumphant proclamation of all that we have learnt. It is sung by the whole congregation standing as their united act of witness to the Faith, and signed by each at the end with the Cross, as their personal signature, and a token that we should not be ashamed to confess this faith of Christ crucified.

The SERMON, for which we sit, brings to a point this preparatory part or " Ante-Communion." It should help the worshipping congregation to enter more fully into the act of worship which follows. At this point too, matters of family interest and importance are announced, such as Banns of Marriage, etc.

The Offertory

After the sermon we come to the Eucharistic Service proper. The Church, gathered together, *does* something as a whole Body before God. What is this? It is an act of sacrifice, and from earliest days the Eucharist has been known as the Christian Sacrifice. The worship of the Christian Church will be an act which *costs*. " I will not offer to the Lord that which costs me nothing." To worship truly is to give rather than to get, so the Church comes together to *offer*. She offers Bread and Wine, and in those elements, without which the service would not be the Eucharist, all her prayers and praises, her own self, the souls and bodies of her members, are focused. It was no accident that our Lord instituted the Sacrament in bread and wine, for they symbolise human life reduced to its simplest expression. An offering of bread and wine thus represents the bringing to God of the whole of human life. The name " Offertory " covers this whole section of the service; the sentences (a relic of the ancient Offertory Psalm) and a hymn; the collection of alms; the solemn offering of the bread and wine; the " Prayer for the Church," in which we ask God to accept our " alms and oblations."

In the earliest liturgies the offerings of the people

were offerings in kind (as still in the mission-field to-day), and were brought to the altar by the congregation; from them the bread and wine for the Eucharist were taken. In our rite the elements are still the people's offering, though for convenience sake they now give money to enable the Church officers to provide the necessary offerings in kind. The offerings are brought up by the people's own representatives, the Wardens, while an OFFERTORY PSALM or Hymn is sung. This act of offering of daily life is summed up in the words of the prayer which follows " for the whole state of Christ's Church." In the name of the offering people, the priest presents their gifts before God, asks Him to accept them, prays that the common offering may express a true unity of spirit, and then sets before Him the labours and needs of the Christian community: the rulers of the State, the bishops and clergy, the faithful laity, especially the congregation present, the sick and sad, remembering finally those departed, members still of the one family in Christ.

From now on the two strands of CONSECRATION and COMMUNION are interwoven. The INVITATION (" Ye that do truly . . ."), CONFESSION, ABSOLUTION and COMFORTABLE WORDS, the PRAYER OF ACCESS (" We do not presume . . .") belong to the second section (Communion), and need no explanation. ALL should join in the CONFESSION.

The Consecration

To the first section belong the SURSUM CORDA (" Lift up your hearts "), SANCTUS and BENEDICTUS, the CONSECRATION PRAYER, the PRAYER OF OBLATION (" O Lord and Heavenly Father . . .")—printed

M

after the actual communion, and the LORD'S PRAYER. This section is called the " Canon," a Greek word meaning a rule, the " rule by which the consecration is properly performed." It begins with thanksgiving; all should *stand* after the Comfortable Words for the SURSUM CORDA and SANCTUS, kneeling again for the PRAYER OF ACCESS and CONSECRATION.

The Consecration expresses in the act what we mean by the words " through Jesus Christ our Lord." The gifts offered at the Offertory, symbolising our lives, our daily work, ourselves, are taken by Christ, who comes to the earthly altar, Himself blesses the offerings, takes them, breaks them, and " consecrates " them, makes them holy, using the priest as His mouthpiece, but himself the Consecrator. In themselves they are unworthy to be offered to His Divine Majesty; we can do nothing to make them worthy, but *He* can, and does, in the Consecration. According to His promise, He is present, and His Presence is the link between earth and heaven. The gong within the church welcomes the Presence and focuses worship; the church bell summons the faithful outside to join in the one act of Godward offering; lights greet the Lord of heaven and earth; and in the still silence that follows the Consecration the only words fit to be uttered by the Church of sinful men approaching so close in Jesus Christ to the Eternal Throne are those of the AGNUS DEI—" O Lamb of God . . . have mercy upon us . . . grant us Thy Peace."

The Communion

During the Agnus Dei, the priest and his attendants receive Communion, and immediately after it the choir. Then during the singing of a COMMUNION PSALM or Hymn, the people come up (*it is better if they come ten at a time, to avoid a queue in the aisle*).

In Communion the gifts offered at the Offertory— her life, her work—and lifted up into Christ's one perfect Offering in the Consecration, are given back to the Church by God, transformed, transfigured. The bread is no longer just common bread, no longer life secular, unsanctified, but the Body of Christ. It is *His* Life, in which all His members share. The gift is given to them not as individuals, but as fellow-members in the Body; they are " communicants," sharers, partakers; for it is through the Body, the society, which is His instrument, that Christ works upon the world. And the gift of His Life is bestowed that it, that they, may become a worthier instrument, more truly and effectively His Body.

The Thanksgiving

After the act of Communion, the first words of common prayer are those of the family prayer of the Church, the OUR FATHER, in which all join. Then follows the PRAYER OF OBLATION or the PRAYER OF THANKSGIVING, and the GLORIA IN EXCELSIS, for which all stand and in which all join. It closes our worship with a united act of triumphant and yet penitent adoration, joining us again with the worship of the angels round the throne of the Lamb in heaven.

So the priest lets us depart with the BLESSING, for which we kneel. What God first gave to us, we have willingly offered to Him. He has accepted its unworthiness " through Jesus Christ," and given it back to us charged with His Life. Strengthened by that

Body, we go forth to enter again upon our calling to be His Body in the world.

A HYMN concludes the service, while the priest and his attendants depart. The priest will conduct a short ACT OF THANKSGIVING immediately after this in the aisle, after which choir and people go out into the world again.

A LAST WORD

By P. N. Waggett, S.S.J.E.

As we come for the peace that we need, as we come round that Table, which is the Supper-Table of our heavenly home, as we come to eat the Bread of Life, Jesus Christ, see that there is pity, see that there is compassion, considerateness, " tarrying one for the other." Here is the true ritual of the Altar. No recovery of ancient symbols, of Catholic ceremonial, will make the sanctuary anything but poor and bare and mean while there is one soul hindered, one soul offended, one man needlessly kept away from the Table of the Lord. Think of that. That is what the Lord desires to see—His Holy Table surrounded by sympathy, courtesy, gentleness, brotherly love, mutual compassion, the cloud of the incense of happy prayer. That is what He requires—the ceremonial of an unfailing courtesy, the richness of a family drawn together round His feet; the true antiquity, the true Catholic dignity of the poor coming where the poor man's friend waits for them. Let us not be content while this holy mystery has around it anything which offends, anything which checks, anything which perplexes.

Let those, therefore, who can love and use the ancient Catholic ceremonial of the Church, be content—as I think they are fully content—that others should still retain the barer worship of our childhood; and let those on the other hand who are offended and checked by things which are practically new although they are historically ancient, let them not grudge a different way to those who are differently moved. And let us all believe that peace is what we want; not uniformity in outward things, but the true harmony of contented hearts; that since one church and one altar cannot possibly in the nature of things present exactly the aspect which all Christians would like to see, but every form must needs offend in some sense some; therefore in the great mansion of God's Church let there be many chambers of approach to the one Bread, that in the midst of a certain diversity of mode we may draw together without check, without alarm, without shame, without debate, with mutual courtesy, tarrying one for the other, in unbroken pity, to Jesus Christ Who is our Peace. Think not that this is too low a thing to have spoken of to-day. Keep it in your prayers. You will be called upon to return presently to the old debates. Refuse them. By the Passion of Jesus, by the mercies of God—I speak to you in God's Name, and you shall hardly be guiltless if you refuse to hear— if there be any consolation in Christ, any love of the Spirit, I will call upon you to avoid all those debates which bring the indignity of discord within sight, within hearing, within thought of the sacred mystery of God's home and the spread table of God's family, into which may He grant to us sinners full entrance for our souls' salvation.

In your silence pray God that you may know your homelessness; pray God to grant you the incoming to His home; pray God to make you, with Mary and all Saints, loyal fellow-brothers and sisters in the great family of Grace.

(From *The Heart of Jesus*; Holy Week addresses in St. Paul's Cathedral, 1901.)

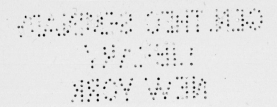

Printed and Bound in Great Britain by
Richard Clay & Sons, Limited,
Bungay, Suffolk.

[6]